"In this focused guide to South Korean business attitudes, manners and procedures, the author has articulated the historical and Confucian roots of Korean society while recognizing the tremendous changes which have taken place in the country over the last quarter century. Now there is truly a "Korean Way" of doing business, a mix of the old and new in this dynamic, successful and globalizing economy. This book is a "must read" for any professional venturing into this complex but rewarding market."

—**Martin H. Sours**, Professor, Global Studies
Thunderbird School of Global Management

"Boyé Lafayette de Mente was writing about how to do business in Asia before contemporary authors of similar books were born. His many decades of experience give valuable insight not only into the vast differences between East and West but within the region as well. *The Korean Way in Business* is one of this author's several well-received volumes on Korea that should be pre-requisite reading for anyone intending to do business there."

—**Steve Herman**, Veteran foreign correspondent in Asia

"Koreans are not like their neighbors China and Japan, they are unique in language, dress, food, and in the way they understand how business should be conducted. If you want to have a chance, it is helpful to know the Korean way."

—**John E. Banta**, CEO, Nongshim Hotel Group

T0151854

Other books by the Author

Books on China

The Chinese Way in Business: Secrets of Successful Business Dealings in China

The Chinese Mind—Understanding Traditional Chinese Beliefs and Their Influence on Contemporary Culture

Chinese in Plain English

Survival Chinese

Instant Chinese

Etiquette Guide to China—Know the Rules that Make the Difference

Books on Japan*

KATA—The Key to Understanding & Dealing with the Japanese

Japan's Cultural Code Words

The Japanese Have a Word for It!

Mistress-Keeping in Japan

Exotic Japan—The Sensual & Visual Pleasures

Discovering Cultural Japan

Business Guide to Japan

Japanese in Plain English

Speak Japanese Today—A Little Language Goes a Long Way!

Instant Japanese

Survival Japanese

Japan Made Easy—All You Need to Know to Enjoy Japan

Dining Guide to Japan

Shopping Guide to Japan

Etiquette Guide to Japan—Know the Rules that Make the Difference

The Japanese Samurai Code—Classic Strategies for Success

Japan Unmasked—The Character & Culture of the Japanese

Elements of Japanese Design— Understanding & Using Japan's Classic *Wabi-Sabi-Shibui* Concepts

Sex and the Japanese—The Sensual Side of Japan

Samurai Strategies—42 Secret Martial Arts from Musashi's "Book of Five Rings"

Asian Face Reading—Unlock the Secrets Hidden in the Human Face

Books on Korea

Korean Business Etiquette

Korean in Plain English

Korea's Business & Cultural Code Words

Etiquette Guide to Korea— Know the Rules that Make the Difference

Instant Korean

Survival Korean

Books on Mexico

Why Mexicans Think & Behave the Way They Do—The Cultural Factors that Created the Character & Personality of the Mexican People

The Mexican Mind – Understanding & Appreciating Mexican Culture

Romantic Mexico—The Image & the Realities

* Some of the Japan titles are also available in Chinese, Czech, French, German, Hebrew, Italian, Indonesian, Japanese, Polish, Portuguese, Russian & Spanish editions.

THE
KOREAN
WAY IN
BUSINESS

Understanding and Dealing with the South Koreans in Business

BOYÉ LAFAYETTE DE MENTE

TUTTLE Publishing

Tokyo | Rutland, Vermont | Singapore

CONTENTS

PREFACE
The Origin of South Korea 8

INTRODUCTION
The Rise of South Korea 10

The Great *Chaebol* Conglomerates...................11
The KOTRA Contribution.................................14
Major Business Centers 15
TV Sales and Internet Shopping......................15
The Corporate Graveyard 15
Foreign Companies in South Korea 15
Opportunities for Green Industries.................16
The Defense Industries 16
Success of the Fast-Food Chains 17
Using Lawyers in South Korea.........................17
Marketing and Sales Infrastructure 18
Business Entertainment Industry.....................18
A Difference in Corporate Philosophy.............18
Other Reasons Why Foreign Companies Fail....19
Getting Help from Chambers of Commerce....20
Getting Help from Private Consultants 21
The "Force" that Drives Koreans 22
Work as Religion 26
The Lust for Power 26
Fighting at the Drop of a Hat 27
The Legacy of Enforced Harmony..................28
The Clans Are Alive and Well 30
The Problem of Names 31
A Primary Contact for Newcomers.................36

CHAPTER ONE
A Historical Profile 38

Early Kingdoms 38
The Last Dynasty 40
Contact with Japan 41
Colonization by Japan 43
The Korean War and Its Aftermath 44

CHAPTER TWO
The Basics of Korean Etiquette & Ethics 46

The Perils of Using Logic 47
The Ethics of Group Consciousness................49
The "Good Mood" Syndrome 50

Dealing with Sensitive Feelings............................51
Dealing with Powerful Emotions.....................52
Avoiding the Appearance of Arrogance 53
Dealing with South Korean Nationalism.......................54
The Western Way vs. the South Korean Way.................55
What is Fair in South Korea?...........................56
The Emotional Content of Business................................57

CHAPTER THREE

The Enduring Korean Character 59

Humanism and Benevolence in Business........................60
Defining South Korean Management 60
"Scold Management" 63
Mind Control 64
Striving for Power 64
The Battle for an Education 65
Etiquette as Morality 66
Dealing with Duty and Obligations 67
Korean-Style Sin 68
The Personal Nature of Business 69
More Personal Elements in Business 72
Respect in South Korea 74
The Personal Loyalty Factor 75
Saving Everybody's Face 76
Hospitality as Face 78
Avoiding Shame 79
The Unbearable Burden 80
The Shame of Failure 81
Death before Dishonor 81
Peace of Mind 82
Situational Truth 83
Justice South Korean Style 84
The Communications Problem 86
The Great Ethical Divide 88
The Kindness Trap 89
Class Consciousness and School Ties 89
Juniors and Seniors 90
The Power of Social Debts 92
The Stubborn Syndrome 92
Doing Things by the Book 93
Dealing with Facts 94
When "Maybe" Means "No" 95
Personal Responsibility 96
Dealing with "Big Brother" 97
The Guiding Hand of Government 99
The Role of Friends in Business 101

The Importance of Sincerity 102
The Self-Reliant Syndrome 103

CHAPTER FOUR
Korean Business Culture Today 105
Manners as Morality 106
Circumstantial Ethics 107
The Perils of *Pipyong* 108
The Ethics of Revenge 109
The Jealousy Virus 110
Honoring Superiors 111
The Social Pecking Order 112
The Faction Syndrome 113
Corporations as Military Units 114
The Rank-Based Society 114
Rank has its Privileges 115
The Military Factor in Business 116
Cold Calls Are Out 117
Appointments and Meetings 118
Office Call Protocol 118
Dressing for Business 119
The Dual Role of Name Cards 120
The Use of First Names 121
Gift Giving vs. Bribery 121
To Bow or Not to Bow? 123
Standing Up at the Right Time 125
Rounds of Greetings 126
The South Korean View and Use of Contracts 127
Big Foreign Company Myopia 132
Major Problem Areas 132
Conflicting Goals 134
Playing Games with the Books 134
Privacy South Korean Style 135
Working for a Boss, Not a Company 135
Female Employees 136
Women and Male Chauvinism 136
The Great Walls of South Korea 137
Disobeying Laws 138
Reading Each Other's *Nunchi* 139
The Role and Importance of Social Status 142
Relationships and Connections 142
Human Harmony in Management 144
Ties that Bind 144
The Importance of a Dignified Manner 146
The Decision-Making System 147
Negotiating South Korean Style 150

Negotiations Dos and Don'ts 151
The Bargaining Factor in Business 153
Controlling Competition 154
Hospitality and Business 154
Private Invitations 156
Business Dining 156
Business Drinking 157
Singing Your Way to Success 160
Having Fun in a *Kisaeng* House 162
The Job Rotation System 164
Company Mottos and Creeds 165
Dealing with Office Stress 166
Advice for Foreign Managers 166
Avoiding Cultural Backlash 167
The Role of "Go-Betweens" 168
The Need for Patience 169
Formula for Keeping Best Workers 170
Developing Team Spirit 170
The Use of Collective Punishment 171
Veterans' Law 171
Foreign Workers 172
Emphasis on Company Training 172
Arbitration Taboos 173
The Importance of the Apology 173
The Korean Adaptation of English 174
Dos and Don'ts 175
Regulation by Competitors 176
The Prime Contact for Newcomers 176
The Good Side 177
A Pending Retirement Law 179

CHAPTER FIVE

Vocabulary of the Korean Way 180

Appendix 1

Management Titles and Their Korean Equivalents 210

Appendix 2

Guide to Korean Pronunciation 212

Index 216

The Origin of South Korea

At the end of World War II in August 1945, the Soviet Red Army took over the northern half of the Korean peninsula and immediately set up a Communist-style military dictatorship under a Korean Communist named Kim Il-sung.

There was no central authority in the southern half of the peninsula and for the next three years the country was embroiled in insurrections and all-out warfare between factions, resulting in the death of over 100,000 people.

Finally, in August 1948, the leading factions agreed to form the Republic of South Korea, with Syngman Rhee, a former political exile, as its president. However, that was not to be the end of strife in South Korea: Rhee assumed dictatorial powers, and came in conflict with ongoing opposition from factions that had different agendas.

In 1949 Rhee initiated a military campaign to kill people suspected of being Communist sympathizers and friendly toward North Korea. The small contingent of American military forces and political advisors still in South Korea at that time did nothing to stop the mayhem. In the spring of 1950, North Korea invaded South Korea in a savage effort to incorporate it into the north's Communist regime. American and allied forces finally intervened, forcing the North Koreans and their Chinese allies back above the 38th parallel, which was the original dividing line between the two countries—and still today divides the peninsula into two countries. Hostilities ended in July 1953, but the Korean War had caused the deaths of millions of Koreans and devastated the country.

This book describes present-day South Korea and relates how its people finally came together with a degree of determination, diligence, energy, and foresight that was astounding—a vivid demonstration of what the people of Korea are capable of when they are free to help themselves.

The Rise of South Korea

The transformation of South Korea from abject poverty to one of the world's most economically, politically, and socially advanced countries in less than 30 years is one of the great stories of the last 50 years; a phenomenon patterned after the incredible rise of Japan following the end of its shogunate era in 1867–68.

South Korea is much smaller than Japan and had to overcome many more challenges—including a devastating civil war with North Korea—in its transformation into a world-class industrial power. This process that can be traced directly to elements of its traditional culture, to government policies, and to the creation of huge conglomerates like the *zaibatsus* that transformed feudal Japan between 1870 and 1890.

Also, like both modern Japan and China, the South Korean way of doing business is a hybrid of traditional cultural elements and Western-style practices that give it many advantages in competing with Western nations.

By the turn of the 21st century the personal lifestyle of South Koreans had been almost completely Westernized in virtually every sense of the word—a lifestyle based on individualism within the normal confines of a society and a competitive economy; and the younger South Koreans in particular are more individualistic in their manner and their lifestyle.

One of the most dramatic examples of the fundamental shift in the mindset and behavior of Koreans was the election of a woman, Park Geun-hye, as president of the country in February 2013. She is the daughter of former Korean president Park Chung-hee, a South Korean army general, who was assassinated in 1979.

On the technological side, the country leads the world in the number of people connected via personal communication devices, and the younger generations are avid users of Internet-based social media, educational programs, and recreational games. Virtually 100 percent of South Korean mobile phones have Internet access.

Broadly speaking, the Internet has a higher status for South Koreans than it does for Westerners—a phenomenon the government actively supports. According to the Information Technology and Innovation Foundation, South Korea is the most Internet-connected country in the world. Seoul, the nation's capital, has been called "the bandwidth capital of the world." It also has the cheapest and the fastest broadband in the world.

South Korea leads the world in a number of industries, including not only telecommunications and such scientific endeavors as stem-cell research but also—and surprisingly enough—in shipbuilding.

The Great *Chaebol* Conglomerates

South Korea became Asia's fourth-largest economy and a major player among the world's top manufacturing and exporting nations between the early 1960s and the 1980s due to the rapid growth of several *chaebols* (chay-bols)—which means "business associations"—combined with the cultural attributes the Korean people had inherited from their past.

In the 1960s the South Korean government teamed up with a number of existing family-owned companies to transform them into huge conglomerates, each with dozens of divisions and branch companies that specialized in a wide range of fields, from automobiles, chemicals, and electronics to shipbuilding.

Among these government-backed economic powerhouses were the Daewoo Group, the Hyundai Group, the Samsung Group, the LG Group, Kia Motors, the SK Group, POSCO (Pohang Iron & Steel), and Ssang Yong. These family-owned and managed *chaebols* were, and still are, responsible for over 50 percent of all the production and exports in South Korea.

There had been large family-owned companies in South Korea before 1960, but when the regime of General Park Chung-hee came into existence in 1961, Park began working directly with these companies to model them after Japan's famous pre-World War II *zaibatsu* conglomerates, which developed during the early years of the Meiji period following the downfall of the shogunate form of government in 1867–68. The *zaibatsus* turned Japan into a manufacturing and exporting powerhouse within 20 years—a phenomenon that South Korean president Park was determined to emulate.

While Japan's *zaibatsu* groups were centered on banks that provided them with capital, Park nationalized all South Korean banks and ordered them to finance the *chaebols* in the pursuit of national goals that he personally directed. While there were some downturns over the next decades, on the whole, the *chaebols* grew at an astounding speed, transforming the country into one of the world's most advanced and dynamic economies.

One of the ways the South Korean government continued to support the *chaebols* was to control the entry of foreign companies into the country and restrict how they operated.

The three largest *chaebols* are Samsung, Hyundai, and LG. These three conglomerates alone account for approximately 30 percent of South Korea's gross national product (GNP).

The largest and most successful of these industrial conglomerates is Samsung, which has become the international face of South Korea. Founded in 1938 as a food exporter selling dried fish and flour to China, the company went into life insurance, textiles, and other businesses during the 1950s and 1960s.

Samsung Electronics was founded in 1969 and began selling

black-and-white TVs in 1970. During the 1970s it added micro-waves, refrigerators, washing machines, and petrochemicals to its lineup. Color TVs, personal computers, tape recorders, and VCRs followed in the 1980s.

In the 1990s Samsung began introducing technological innovations to its products and launched a marketing program to dramatically increase its exports to the United States. The company introduced its first flagship Android phone, the Galaxy S, at the Mobile World Congress in 2010.

In April 2013 Samsung Electronics introduced a version of its smartphone that does not require touching the screen to use it. The phone reacts to the movement of the eyes. Japan's NTT DoCoMo was reported as testing the same technology on its tablets. Industry watchers dubbed the eye-movement technology "the third interface"—after fingers and voice.

Samsung has continued to increase its dominance in the IT field not only by introducing technological innovations and new products but by becoming multinational in its operation. LG (originally named Lucky and Goldstar) followed the same electronics path to world renown as Samsung.

In 2013 Samsung Electronics opened 1,400 direct sales outlets in the U.S.'s Best Buy chain of electronic stores. The outlets, called Samsung Experience Shops, are managed by Samsung employees. In addition to offering Samsung products they also offer customer support. Samsung products were already being sold in Best Buy stores but were stocked in different departments of the stores.

All of South Korea's *chaebols* came under strong criticism during the first decade of the 21st century, with its critics pointing out that the huge corporations prevented the development and growth of other companies. But the government was reluctant to take a stand against the *chaebols* because they were so important to the economy.

Some observers of South Korean society say that changes in the mindset and behavior of the people will ultimately erode the monopolistic power of the *chaebols*. They presently employ about 25 percent of the workforce of South Korea and produce about 50 percent of its industrial output. They also represent the positive and negative sides of the hold that the traditional culture has on the people of South Korea, and for the time being they will remain the face of South Korea and a portent of its future.

Despite the domination of South Korea's economy by these huge industrial conglomerates—or perhaps because of them—the country as a whole is widely regarded as both a showcase and a model for the future.

The KOTRA Contribution

In conjunction with the *chaebols* the South Korean government in 1962 established the Korea Trade-Investment Promotion Corporation as a national trade promotion organization. In 1995 the name was changed to the Korean Trade-Investment Agency (KOTRA), which has since engaged in a variety of trade promotion activities overseas, including match-making and providing support for foreign companies interested in investing in South Korea.

KOTRA has pursued the twin goals of attracting foreign investment into South Korea and promoting the manufacturing and export industries designed to make the country the business and economic hub of Southeast Asia. The agency has well over a hundred Korean Business Centers in 78 countries and over a dozen offices in South Korea. One of the first steps that foreign companies planning on doing business in South Korea can take is to contact the nearest office of KOTRA.

(Foreigners who want to work in South Korea should get in touch with Contact Korea, a service provided by KOTRA.)

Another way the South Korean government contributed to the economy was approving the development of free trade zones. By the turn of the century there were six Free Economic Zones that provided all of the business and personal needs of the people who worked there, from housing, schools, and hospitals to shopping and entertainment facilities. These six zones are Busan Jinhae, Daegu Gyeonbuk, Gwangyang, Incheon, Saemangum Gunsan, and Yellow Sea.

Major Business Centers

Most of South Korea's major companies clustered in eight business centers: Seoul; Busan (formerly known as Pusan); Incheon, which adjoins the Seoul metropolitan area and was South Korea's first Free Economic Zone; Ulsan and the east coast area, where the shipbuilding industry is centered; the bio center of Osong, south of Seoul; the large metro area of Daegu; the high-tech and international center of Songdo near Incheon; Yeongjong, near Incheon International Airport; and the sports-oriented city of Cheongas.

These business centers were natural magnets for the first foreign enterprises in the country.

TV Sales and Internet Shopping

With the introduction of TV shopping in South Korea in 1996, TV quickly became an important factor in product sales. This was followed by Internet shopping, with well over 2,000 cyber shopping malls appearing as if by magic. Some of the malls offered 3-D views of the products and others began live broadcasting. These venues have offered a variety of opportunities to foreign companies.

The Corporate Graveyard

The South Korean government policies created by the Park regime created what some have referred to as a "graveyard" for foreign companies—that is, it required foreign companies to follow policies that virtually guaranteed many of them would fail.

One of the most significant of these barriers was the rights and privileges of South Korean labor unions. They made it difficult, and sometimes impossible, to hire and fire employees. The tactics of the unions were conducted like military campaigns, where the only acceptable outcome is victory.

Virtually all of the foreign companies that have failed in South Korea did so because their managers could not establish mutually-agreeable relationships with their employees and their unions.

Foreign Companies in South Korea

Despite governmental and cultural obstacles, by the end of the

20th century there were over 12,000 foreign firms operating in South Korea, and the number has continued to grow. Most of these firms are in consumer product fields, from apparel, food, and drinks to high-end fashions. Some of these companies went into South Korea through agents and distributors; others through licensing and franchising.

Not surprisingly, most foreign-owned and operated enterprises in South Korea were created outside the realm of the *chaebols*, but they face many of the same cultural factors that apply to virtually all South Koreans in the management of their businesses and in the necessary relationships they have with government officials on all levels.

According to surveys by American and European organizations high-growth opportunities in South Korea include aerospace, product design and development, and all of the consumer and industrial electronics areas. Other areas that are considered worth looking into include automobiles, consumer products of all kinds, education advances, the energy industries, environmental concerns, financial and legal matters, and life sciences.

Opportunities for Green Industries

The South Korean government has a number of programs designed to benefit foreign companies wanting to bring environmentally-friendly firms into the country. These programs include grants and are administered by the Foreign Investment Promotion Act. Foreign companies in this category can get further information from KOTRA's Korean Business Centers.

The Defense Industries

South Korea has an enormous defense industry that engages in business in a variety of fields, including exporting. While the defense industry may offer some opportunities to foreign companies, the competition is fierce. There is a sizeable cadre of agents who specialize in dealing with the defense industry, and some of them represent foreign clients. Their names are readily available in Seoul telephone directories and business journals.

Success of the Fast-Food Chains

Interestingly, American fast-food chains have been among the most successful foreign companies in South Korea, primarily because their impact on the nation's economy is minimal. South Korea imports 60–70 percent of its food and drink products and the two combined are one of the largest industrial segments in the country.

As of the time of writing, foreign fast-food chains in South Korea include Baskin-Robbins, Bennigan's, Burger King, California Pizza Kitchen, Cold Stone, Domino's Pizza, Dunkin' Donuts, Johnny Rockets, Kentucky Fried Chicken, Krispy Kreme, Hooters, Jamba Juice, McDonald's, Mister Donut, On The Border, Outback Steakhouse, Papa John's, Pizza Hut, Popeyes, Quiznos, Sizzler, Smoothie King, Starbucks, Subway, Taco Bell, TGI Friday's, Tony Roma's, and Uno Chicago Grill.

Using Lawyers in South Korea

Many foreign companies operating in South Korea resort at one time or another to hiring attorneys, with mixed results. Stories about the incompetence of Korean lawyers who cause more problems than they solve abound in the foreign business community. Some critics say that as many as 70 percent of the attorneys in the country are incompetent. So it is wise to select law firms and attorneys only on the basis of trustworthy recommendations from people who know what they are talking about.

Copious information about South Korea's laws are available in English on the Internet. One primary source for such information is available from www.korea.net/government/government.html.

The Korean Ministry of Employment and Labor oversees issues involving employment conditions, industrial relations, accident protection, welfare promotion, job security, and vocational training. Information about this Ministry is also available in English.

For specific details about hiring and firing of employees in South Korea under the Labor Standards Act, see an online English language translation of the Act at www.ilo.org/dyn/natlex/docs/WEBTEXT/46401/65062/E98KORO1.htm

Marketing and Sales Infrastructure

South Korea has all of the usual marketing and sales promotion media and techniques, including sponsoring popular sports organizations. There are also the usual government agencies for protecting intellectual property. All of the typical recruiting channels for new employees are also available in South Korea, including newspapers, trade journals, and recruitment agencies that specialize in all of the country's main industrial areas.

Business Entertainment Industry

In order to function efficiently in South Korea expatriate foreign businessmen must be well-versed in the business-oriented entertainment industries that range from "low class" to "high class." These include "stand bars" and karaoke bars (*noraebang* / no-rye-bahng), in which the hostesses "know how to handle men;" and lower and upper class "business clubs." The lower-class business clubs, *danranjujeom* (dahn-rahn-juu-jome), feature private rooms where the patrons and the hostesses can let their hair down.

The highest class of entertainment for business men is provided by swanky "business clubs" that are also referred to as "room salons." The hostesses in these clubs are usually younger and prettier, and are often invited out by their patrons on dinner dates and trysts.

A Difference in Corporate Philosophy

There is a fundamental difference in the corporate philosophies of Western and large South Korean companies. The foundation of Western companies is based on profit-making, pure and simple. In contrast to this the *chaebols* were charged with a second responsibility: contributing directly to the nation-building goals of the government. There are thus three stakeholders in South Korean companies: their employees, their shareholders, and the country at large. One of Samsung's mottos is: "We do business for the sake of nation building!"—something you would never hear from an American or European company.

Other Reasons Why Foreign Companies Fail

One of the most important factors in the problems encountered by foreign companies in South Korea is that the tastes of Koreans are typically different from that of Westerners and cannot be quickly or easily changed. This especially applies to such personal-use products as coffee mixes, cosmetics, formula milk for babies, and personal sanitary items for women.

Generally, the larger the foreign company, the longer it takes for them to recognize the problem and come up with a solution—if they ever do. Even more important is the fact that as soon as individual Korean entrepreneurs and companies see foreign products succeeding in the marketplace, they jump on the bandwagon, typically making improvements that Korean consumers responded to by changing and/or adding new ingredients.

One good example of this is when LG's Unicharm division noted that the sales of foreign-made shampoos, sanitary napkins, and baby diapers were taking off they added traditional herbal ingredients to the products and began powerful advertising programs to promote them. An LG staffer said that after they added the new ingredients to their sanitary napkins their brand quickly became number two in the country, accounting for 30 percent of LG Unicharm's sales.

Korean coffee mix makers began selling boxes with 50 packets instead of the 10 offered by foreign companies. The gambit worked. The Korean coffee mix makers also held monthly taste tests to keep abreast of the preferences of consumers—something the foreign companies could not or did not do. Korean manufacturers of baby formula milk also made dramatic inroads in that market by shifting from the high fat and carbohydrate formulas of American and European versions to lean formulas.

The leading Korean producer of shampoos and rinses was number three in the market when it started putting traditional herbal ingredients into its products. In no time, it shot to number one. The company also began giving complimentary samples of its products to consumers, tripling its daily sales of detergents. Foreign companies that cannot, or do not, learn these lessons do not fare well in South Korea.

Another factor in the success rate of foreign companies in South Korea is their ability, or lack of, to deal effectively with the prevailing cultural traits of Koreans. Many foreigners—Americans in particular—automatically assume that they do not have to change their way of thinking and doing business with Koreans who can communicate in English, shake hands enthusiastically, laugh at their jokes, and make convivial drinking companions.

Many of the cultural traits that control the overall thinking, expectations, and behavior of Koreans are also so subtle they are not easily recognized by Westerners, much less understood and appreciated.

One of the things that top Japanese company owners and managers did in the 1950s and top Korean company owners and managers did in the 1960s was to send their sons and other young employees to the countries they wanted to do business with to study the languages and cultures for up to three years, with absolutely no direct work-related duties to perform.

When these newly-minted bilingual and bicultural employees returned to their companies they were fast-tracked to the top of their firms. The advantages this farsighted practice gave to Japanese and Korean corporations is obvious. And the fact that American and other Western companies did not initiate or imitate this practice is a sign of short-sighted cultural arrogance that has been too costly to imagine.

South Korea's rapid rise to economic prominence was also greatly enhanced by the return of Koreans raised and educated abroad. The language and cultural skills of these returnees, referred to as *gyopo* (g-yoh-poh), which may be translated as "expatriates," made an enormous contribution to the country.

In any given year there are dozens of young South Korean executives enrolled in special short-term executive classes at the Thunderbird School of Global Management in the U.S., in Glendale, Arizona.

Getting Help from Chambers of Commerce*
Foreign chambers of commerce in South Korea are primary sources for detailed and current information about the South

Korean business scene, and provide valuable aid to both members and newcomers. Here is a list of foreign chambers of commerce in Seoul:

- American Chamber Of Commerce (AmCham)
- Australia Chamber Of Commerce In Korea (AustCham)
- British Chamber Of Commerce In Korea (BCCK)
- Canadian Chamber Of Commerce Korea (CanCham)
- China Council For The Promotion Of International Trade
- Dutch Business Club Korea
- European Chamber Of Commerce In Korea (ECCK)
- French-Korean Chamber Of Commerce Korea
- (Irish) Asia-Ireland Chamber Of Commerce
- Italian Chamber Of Commerce In Korea (ITCCK)
- Korean-Swedish Association
- Korean-German Chamber Of Commerce And Industry
- New Zealand Chamber Of Commerce In Korea (Kiwi Chamber)
- Seoul Japan Club
- South African Business Chamber In Korea
- Swedish Chamber Of Commerce In Korea (SCCK)
- Swiss Korean Business Council

*This list was provided by info@korea4expats.com, which also provides current contact information.

Getting Help from Private Consultants

There are numerous consulting firms that can help foreign companies navigate the steps necessary to start doing business in South Korea, and having a better chance of success once they are in.

Over a dozen of these firms have websites. Some of them are located in South Korea; others are in the U.S. and elsewhere. For the names and contact addresses of these firms just Google "business consulting firms in South Korea."

One of these consulting services consists of a group of American attorneys and professionals stationed in Seoul who are members of the full-service international-focused law firm IPG Legal, headquartered in Minneapolis, Minnesota.

IPG works with both Fortune 500 companies and small enterprises. The company has six global offices, and specializes in Asia. It does business in English, Korean, Mandarin, Cantonese, Tagalog, and Khmer.

IPG attorneys offer services in arbitration; asset protection and management; corporate law and compliance; dispute resolution and compliance; energy and mining; international business transactions; infrastructure and development; FDI and free trade zones; franchise and retail; intellectual property; joint venture dispute resolution; mergers and acquisitions; real estate development; SME market entry; and taxation and customs. The IPG office in Seoul is located in the Hong Woo Building.

IPG sponsors *The Korean Law Blog* on the Internet, which provides regular updates on the legal status of business in South Korea. To access, go to: www.korealawblog.com. The current edition of the blog contains authoritative articles on the following topics: Terminate/Layoff of Employees in Korea; Korean Independent Contractor Risks under Korea LSA; The Ten Commandments of Labor Relations in Asia; Korean Labor Relations, by Tom Coyner; There Goes the Neighborhood: Samsung "Union" Allowed to Protest in Front of Samsung.

The "Force" that Drives Koreans

From the beginning of their history the common people of Korea lived under authoritarian-type regimes that generally prevented them from thinking and behaving as individuals, and dramatically limited their choices in how and where they lived.

With the introduction of Confucianism into Korea over 2,000 years ago (around 108 B.C.), restrictions on individual thought and behavior gradually became more onerous. When the Choson dynasty was established in 1392, it adopted an even more restrictive form of neo-Confucianism that totally controlled the lives of the people, requiring them to repress virtually all of the emotions, spirit, intellect, and ambitions that are inherent in human beings.

In brief, the form of Confucianism adopted by the new Choson dynasty in 1392 and in the decades that followed emphasized what has been called a "father culture." It gave fathers absolute authority over their families, made ancestor worship the primary religion, and required unquestioned obedience to fathers, father figures and government officials, combined with unqualified respect for seniors and elders in general.

This system, which lasted until 1945, built up in the psyche of Koreans a powerful "force" that Korean sociologists refer to as *han* (hahn) or "unrequited resentments"—a force that could be equated to the pressure that builds up in a pot of boiling water that is kept so tightly covered that no steam can escape.

The sociologists go on to say that during Korea's long feudal era there were many kinds of *han*—the *han* of political abuse, the *han* of sexual abuse, the *han* of poverty, the *han* of wartime suffering, the *han* of class immobility, and so on—all of the institutionalized limitations on the freedom to be individuals and hardships Koreans had to endure over the ages.

Described another way, *han* refers to the build up of unrequited yearnings that were created by oppressive religious and political systems; by life in a society in which most of the normal human drives were subverted or totally denied; by a state of constant fear of offending someone; and by intense and permanent feelings of frustration, repressed anger, regret, remorse, grief, deprivation, and helplessness.

By law and by custom, pre-modern Korea's political and social systems kept the people sealed up in cages that prevented them from developing even a fraction of their potential. They became like steel springs that were pressed nearly flat, with few approved ways to release their energy, curiosity, or creativity.

Korean poetry abounds because it was one of the few ways that the people could express themselves without breaking any of the social customs or laws, and it is replete with expressions of *han*—deep feelings of sadness, frustration, and resentment.

About the only personal initiative allowed during the long Choson dynasty (1392–1910) was that sponsored by a few of the reigning Choson kings, the greatest of which was King Sejong. He sponsored a large group of scholars and scientists at a research institute, and personally oversaw the creation of a script for writing the South Korean language, which up to that time had been written using Chinese characters, and which is now regarded as one of the simplest, clearest, and most scientific of all writing systems. There are 10 vowels and 14 consonants in the alphabet, which are combined to form the numerous syllables that make up individual words. (And unlike Chinese characters, which takes years to master, Korea's *Hangul* alphabet can be learned in a day or so.)

As long as the power of Korea's feudal dynasties was sufficient to keep the people in a vice that controlled virtually every thought and action, they appeared to be passive and content. But when this power weakened, as it did periodically, they would explode in violence. Nothing angered, frustrated, and humiliated the proud Koreans more, or added more to their *han* burden, than the occupation and colonization of their country by Japan in 1910.

When Koreans were finally freed in 1953 from the compression chamber in which they had existed for so long, they turned their unleashed ambition, creativity, and energy into building an economic and social superpower in one generation.

Foreigners dealing with South Korea today should be aware of the powerful feelings that continue to drive them. The extraordinary energy they bring to their education system, to their work, and to their determination to succeed, is still fueled by the great psychic bang that occurred when they were finally freed from the physical and mental cage they lived in for so long. (South Korea spends approximately seven percent of its GNP on education—one of the highest rates in the world.)

Despite fundamental changes in the South Korean mindset and behavior over the last half of the 20th century, the teachings of Confucius, the ancient Chinese sage, remains visible in South Korean culture, and must be taken into account in virtually all dealings with South Koreans, including those who have become partially Westernized.

Young South Koreans dress and generally act like Americans, for example, but still the prevailing social system includes many facets of traditional Confucianism—close-knit families, a powerful compulsion to achieve the highest possible education, mutual responsibility for the welfare of the family and relatives, and ongoing respect for seniors.

Ethnically, Koreans belong to the Mongolian race, but their language and culture differ fundamentally from that of the Chinese, Japanese, and Mongolians.

All Koreans speak the same language with only minor regional variations. In South Korea the Korean language has been both the primary reservoir of the traditional culture, and the vehicle that sustains it and passes it on from one generation to the next. Key words in the language serve as windows to the heart, soul, and mindset of the people.

I suggest that no one can fully understand South Koreans, or fully appreciate South Korean culture, without being relatively fluent in the Korean language. The South Korean pattern of thinking and the national character is directly related to the language, not only in its use as a routine communications medium, but in all of the nuances of the culture. North Koreans, on the other hand, have been reprogrammed in a different culture.

Since mastering the Korean language and all of its cultural components is a major challenge—and one that foreign businesspeople stationed in South Korea did not begin to take seriously until the 1990s—the best preliminary option is to become familiar with key words that provide insight into the heart and soul of South Koreans.

In fact, one cannot function properly in South Korean society today without knowing the right words to use for specific occasions, and precisely how to use them. The correct choice that the speaker has to make in vocabulary covers virtually every aspect of society—gender, age, position, class, the circumstances of the moment, and so on.

To paraphrase one Korean language authority: The Korean language is designed to reveal and maintain the social status of speakers. In any conversation, who is the inferior and who is the superior quickly becomes obvious. Because Koreans have become so sensitized to language it is extremely important for people to use humble and modest expressions to avoid offending anyone.

This authority adds that Koreans are "slaves" to the demands of language etiquette. Circumstances are, however, changing, albeit slowly, with the times.

Korean language authorities also note that it ranges from difficult to impossible to speak logically in Korean because the language is designed to be vague, and lacks sufficient abstract terms. Because of this, they continue, a great deal of the communication between Koreans is based on intuition, "reading" the other person's mind, and verbal cues, rather than precise verbalization.

In addition to a special form of polite or honorific speech that is used when addressing superiors and in a variety of formal situations, there are six recognized Korean dialects in different areas of the country, plus a form of Korean that is known as "crude language," which is used by people who are generally outside the pale of normal society.

Work as Religion

One of the legacies of Confucianism that played an extraordinarily positive role in the emergence of South Korea as one of the world's leading economic powers is the convergence of many of the teachings of Confucius into a work ethic and drive for success that is astounding.

In fact, modern-day South Koreans have converted Confucianism, with much of its discipline and group-consciousness, into a work cult. Once they were free to better themselves, getting an education and getting ahead became the primary goals in all Koreans' lives, and they continue to pursue these goals with religious-like fervor.

The Lust for Power

Another aspect of modern-day South Korean culture that impacts on the prevailing ethics is a passion for success and *him* (heem), power that is so common that it can aptly be described as a South Korean trait. This syndrome is a legacy of the long centuries when all power in the country was in the hands of the upper-class elite that administered the affairs of the country.

When the government system that had divided the country into social classes and relegated all authority and power to the upper class—and to fathers in all classes—was abolished, it brought about a true social, economic, and political emancipation for the bulk of the population.

Virtually for the first time in the history of the Korean people, everyone was free to pursue success and power to whatever degree they wanted and were capable of achieving. They had never had the power to control their lives, and the energy released by this newly-achieved freedom provided a dynamism and creativity that had never before existed in the country—a phenomenon that was completely reversed by the new Communist leaders of North Korea.

The passion for *him*, combined with a fierce pride in country, drove South Koreans to get the best possible education, the best possible jobs, and to work with uncommon diligence and energy.

The resulting drive for power not only became one of the primary factors in the national character of South Koreans, it became the foundation for the country's subsequent rise to economic prominence.

Fighting at the Drop of a Hat

History books on Korea have made a big deal about an ancient Chinese description of the country as "The Land of Morning Calm." This line was written by a Chinese observer who was impressed with the utter calmness of the South Korean countryside bathed in the early morning light (with fog covering the tops of nearby hills).

In more recent centuries, early Western visitors to Korea repeatedly commented on the calmness of the people and the lack of violence. These commentators did not bother to add that Koreans were typically calm and passive because the culture, the society, and the government did not sanction any other kind of behavior, and used draconian measures to enforce passivity and calmness.

The fact is, individual Koreans, both men and women, often exploded into violence of one kind or another when they could no longer keep the repressed emotions and desires bottled-up.

With men, this violence usually took the form of drinking to excess and then fighting. In fact, in the early days of the Choson dynasty, public *chontu* (chohn-tuu), or fights, were so common among men that the government issued an edict that men would wear heavy ceramic hats rather than hats made of horsehair, and if they got into a brawl and their hat fell off they would be severely punished.

The volume of violence in Korea diminished dramatically for a number of decades, but the heavy hats were so inconvenient that the government became lax in enforcing the edict, and the policy finally withered away. (It seems logical that the common Western saying, "fight at the drop of a hat," may have actually originated in Korea!)

When Japan occupied Korea in 1910 a Japanese military man wrote that Korean men were more interested in singing and poetry than in fighting. (Korea had an elite class of professional warriors long before Japan had its samurai, but the Korean warriors spent most of their time performing arts, rather than fighting.) In reality, large numbers of Koreans resisted the Japanese occupation, hiding out in the mountains and fighting as guerillas. Others who were forced to work for the Japanese did all they could to sabotage the efforts of the occupiers to eliminate Korean culture.

But centuries of oppression under the Confucian and Japanese regimes did not destroy the spirit of Koreans, and once they were free, their spirits soared. Today, typical Koreans will, in fact, fight at the drop of a hat, to defend their "face," their honor, and their country.

The Legacy of Enforced Harmony

The first reference to the country of Korea was apparently made in a Chinese document, written some 4,000 years ago, that described the people living on the Korean peninsula as peaceful in their demeanor, with precise rules of etiquette that attested to the importance of *hwa* (whah), or harmony, in their society.

The culture of the Koreans at that time revolved around shamanistic beliefs that controlled their daily behavior, from interpersonal relationships between the sexes and the obligations of the people to superiors through to their agricultural activities.

Some 2,000 years later a dramatic event occurred. In 108 B.C. China, with its vastly more advanced civilization, invaded and virtually colonized the Korean peninsula. The Chinese overlords quickly introduced Koreans to their arts and crafts as well as to Buddhism and Confucianism, both of which were to have a fundamental influence on Korean life.

Within a few generations, Buddhism had replaced many of the shamanistic rituals and customs of the Koreans and become the dominant religion on the peninsula. But as the centuries went by, organized Buddhism became so corrupt that it threatened the survival of the kingdoms, resulting in a bloody rebellion against the huge number of militant priests and their fortified monasteries.

With the power of the Buddhists broken, the winners of the rebellion established a new government based on Confucian principles. In 1392, the founders of the Choson dynasty (which was to endure until 1910), applied a new, extremely rigid form of Confucianism as the basis for a new set of laws that prescribed every aspect of etiquette and ethics.

The rigid social system created by the Choson court was designed to ensure absolute *hwa* in society—something with which the Koreans were already familiar, but in this case the laws were among the most repressive ever imposed on any people.

This social system was to prevail in Korea until near the end of the 19th century, by which time the ruling family and its ministers had become as corrupt as the ancient Buddhist priests, had begun to lose control of the country, and had come under the influence of the Japanese, Russians, and Europeans. In 1910 Japan took the extraordinary step of occupying and annexing the country, turning it into a province administered by the Japanese military.

Korea was freed from Japanese occupation in 1945, but the Confucian-based lifestyle of the vast majority of South Koreans did not really begin to change until the 1950s and 1960s. Even today, the influence of over 500 years of programming in Confucian etiquette and ethics is still present in South Korean culture, and cannot be escaped or ignored.

Hwa, or harmony, is still the ideal in South Korean society, but here again this does not mean the universal kind of emotional, spiritual, intellectual, and physical harmony that the term denotes in English. It means South Korean-style harmony—that is, the kind of harmony that results from obeying all of the dictates of the etiquette and ethics now prevailing in South Korean society—etiquette and ethics that have their roots in Confucianism.

While it is true that South Korea's younger generation have thrown off most of the heavier cultural chains that bound their parents and ancestors, enough of the traditional Confucian attitudes and behavior remains to give present-day South Korean culture a flavor of its own that is generally different enough from Western values and behavior that they do not naturally mesh, making it necessary for the two sides to compromise in order to communicate effectively and work together.

The Clans Are Alive and Well

While foreign businesspeople might think that Korea's traditional clan system is ancient history and is not something that they need to concern themselves about, that is not always the case.

Like most ancient nations, Korea began as a collection of clans that gradually coalesced into tribal states and finally unified kingdoms, but in the case of Korea, the orignal *chok* (choak), or "clans," did not gradually disappear over time. Korea's clans survived into modern times because the influence of shamanism, Confucianism, and Buddhism worked against radical changes in society, and contributed to virtually all positions of authority in a clan being monopolized by the leading family, thus ensuring that the goal of each clan was its own survival within the existing kingdoms.

There are said to be 39 "root" clans in South Korea, but more than 2,000 years ago most of the peninsula was controlled by about a dozen clans. The two largest of the clans were the Kim and Yi (the latter clan also spelled as Lee and Rhee). Today, the Kim family has 32-branch clans and accounts for some one-quarter of the population of the country. The Lee family has five branches.

In South Korea the Kims and Lees have remained the most prominent family clans since ancient times, and still today their numerous members dominate much of the economy, the politics, education, and society in general. The family registers of these two clans go back 2,500 years.

While anti-discrimination laws are in place and discrimination may be denied, a person's clan affiliations and place of birth are important factors in education and employment in South Korea—just as regional and racial factors still play a role in the lives of Americans.

Foreign employers in South Korea should be aware of the subtleties involved in "mixing" workers from different clans, and take steps to prevent friction from developing. Again, not surprisingly, the younger the people involved, the less likely they are to be clan conscious.

The Problem of Names

One of the most unusual aspects of South Korean society created by the prominence of a small number of clans over the centuries, and one that also plays a vital role in business as well as all other areas of society, are Korean names. Altogether there are only about 300 *song* (song) or family names in South Korea. The four largest and most influential of the family clans were—and still are—Kim, Pak (Park), Lee, and Choi.

Other major family clans included the Choe, Chung, Kang, Cho, Yun, Chang (Jang), and Rim. Today approximately half of all South Koreans are named Kim, Lee or Park. The eight additional names account for another 15 percent of the population.

Many of the 300 or so family names in South Korea are offshoots of the founding families. Immigrants from China and Mongolia brought in some of the other names.

This unusual name situation is said to derive from the fact that the names of the families that gave birth to the Korean population became imbued with a sacred quality that was assiduously maintained from one generation to the next. Confucianism incorporated the concept of revering one's ancestors, which further encouraged the maintenance of the family name and negated any inclination to adopt a new surname that would have no history and no honor.

It has also long been the custom for each Korean to have two given names—one a personal name and the other a generational name, chosen by the parents, grandparents, or an onomancer (name-giver). A male generational name is given to the first son born in a family, and a female generational name is given to the first daughter. Thereafter all additional sons and daughters in the family are given the same generational names.

As the family branches out over the generations, the generational names are continued in the male and female lines, so that eventually people who are very distantly related may have a common generational name that goes back to a remote ancestor.

Because of the special, almost mystical, role that names played in traditional Korean society, people were very sensitive about their names, and there were numerous taboos about using them. In earlier times, many Koreans were so sensitive about their personal names that they did not like to hear other people say them aloud.

Still today, a great deal of thought goes into the selection of both personal names and generational names, and it is still common for parents to seek the help of professional name-givers. The object is to select a name that fits the child on the basis of the time it was born and the parents' expectations for the child.

Among South Koreans, only family members and close school friends address each other by their first names. Foreigners should not address new South Korean contacts by their first names until a proper relationship has been established, and only then if their age and their social and professional status are roughly equal—and this reminder especially applies to Americans, who are culturally programmed to equate the use of first names with equality and sincerity. Young people, including those in positions of authority, should not address older people by their first names.

South Korean women do not change their names when they marry. They may be called by their maiden name, by the title of *puin* (puu-een) or *ojumoni* (oh-juu-moe-nee), both meaning "wife," or as "the wife of Mr Lee," etc.

To get around the extraordinary problem created by the fact that every other South Korean is either Kim, Lee, Pak, or Choi,

South Koreans use titles connected with their profession, place of work, and rank. In companies where there are dozens to hundreds of Lees, Kims, Paks, and Chois, individuals are usually identified by their titles, along with their sections or divisions. If there are two or more Manager Lees in one section they may be referred to as Manager Lee of Production No. 1; Manager Lee of Production No. 2; and so on.

"Names are indeed a horrendous problem," noted long-time Seoul resident Carole Alexander. "In one department (of the Westin Chosun Hotel) we had two Lees. We called one 'Senior Lee' and the other one 'Baby Lee'." On the personal side, South Koreans also use the areas where they live to identify each other.

Many of the most common names in South Korea may be spelled two or three different ways. Some of the syllables making up the South Korean language are also pronounced differently by many people, making the names sound different, especially to foreign ears that are not totally sensitized to the variations in the language.

This name situation creates special problems for foreigners who are newly arrived in South Korea and who try to telephone people they have recently met. Not being aware of the seriousness of the situation, they frequently fail to understand or remember the titles and sections or departments of the people concerned, and are therefore unable to identify which Lee, Choi, Pak, or Kim they want to talk to.

South Koreans who have been educated abroad or have had substantial experience with Westerners in South Korea have become accustomed to foreigners calling them Mr, Mrs, or Miss, and it is becoming more commonplace for them to also use these Western titles when addressing each other, especially when they do not know the individual's proper South Korean title.

It is very important for foreign travelers and businessmen visiting South Korea to carefully write down the full name, title (if any), and company section of all South Koreans whom they might want to call or meet again. On a personal level, it is also wise to get their home addresses and often their position in the family (first or second son or daughter, etc.). The name problem is one of the primary reasons why name-cards are so important in doing business in South Korea.

Until recent years, traditional-minded South Koreans were extraordinarily sensitivity about the use of first names. Before they could make a decision to use a foreign first name, for example, they often had family meetings and discussed the matter endlessly, with a seriousness that astounds the uninitiated foreigner.

Said one veteran foreign businessman in Seoul: "We had one man who worked for us for fifteen years, and was known by everyone as 'Ted.' I met his daughter one day and was amazed to discover that she did not know her father had a foreign nickname."

Commented another foreign businessman: "In my seventeen years in South Korea I have been able to develop close, first-name relationships with only five South Koreans. I recall that when I first arrived here, the American ambassador advised me that it would take me one year to get to know a South Korean, two years before they would accept me (if I didn't make any terrible mistakes), and three years before I would be able to get any work done.

"The ambassador's timetable proved to be painfully accurate. U.S. companies that assign managers here for only two or three years are wasting time and money. Friendship and trust must be built up on both sides, and if it is solid it will last a lifetime. Once you have established this kind of relationship with South Koreans, they will never forget you, and will do everything they can to maintain the relationship."

Personal names are one of the great inventions of humanity, and family names are now so important to life in communities that it is hard to image living in a society in which the vast majority of people do not have family names.

But that was the case in Korea. Men in the commoner class were not allowed to have family names until near the end of the 19th century, and females in the same class were not granted the right until 1909.

A growing number of men, especially among those involved in international business of any kind, choose to go by the initial letters of their given names to make it easier for foreigners to understand and use. Chong Chill Kim becomes C. C. Kim. Other families that have become international in their lifestyle dispense with the generational name altogether.

Another variation in the presentation of given and generational names that has been adopted by some English language news publications in South Korea is to connect the two names with a hyphen, and begin the generational name with a small letter instead of a capital, i.e. Chong-chill.

The small number of family names in South Korea causes identity problems among South Koreans themselves, so it is easy to imagine how much more difficult it can be for foreigners to keep the Kims, Lees, Paks (or Parks) straight.

In personal situations, it is common for people to use the district they live in, or their actual address, to help identify individuals. And it is sometimes necessary to use the family birth rank (first son, second son) to identify someone.

Foreign businesspeople visiting South Korea or having South Korean guests should, of course, make sure they get the name cards of individuals they meet, and if there is not enough information on the cards to distinguish them, ask for more and write it down on the back of the card. (Not too long ago, name cards were held in such high esteem that it was considered bad form to write on them, but this cultural taboo is fading away.)

Because of the serious problem of distinguishing between so many people with the same last name, it is becoming more common for people to adopt *pyolmyong* (pyole-m'yong), or nicknames. Once you become acquainted with someone it is appropriate to ask if they have a nickname.

It is also still the rule for South Koreans to use *tojang* (toe-jahng), or name seals, in lieu of signing their names on ordinary letters or documents. Seals that are used for stamping official documents must be registered with the local authorities, and are known as *ingan* (een-gahn).

There are also other aspects of South Korea's traditional culture that have survived into modern times that must be recognized and understood for one to interact effectively with South Koreans in business and in other areas—again, particularly for those who are having to deal with government agencies and the laws of the country. It is also necessary to keep up with changes in old laws and new ones.

Both business and social etiquette in today's South Korea remains far more formal than what is common in the United States, for example, and this formality represents a society in which the people are typically better behaved, more honest, and more trustworthy than people in Western countries.

A Primary Contact for Newcomers

The American Chamber of Commerce in South Korea (AmCham) is a primary source of information and guidance on the mechanics of doing business in the country. The chamber notes that the South Korean business environment has undergone enormous changes since the late 1990s, with a huge number of regulations amended or wiped off the books altogether, and the process continues. The Chamber adds that South Korea is more open to, and welcoming of, international business than it has ever been in the past.

South Korea, continues AmCham, is a highly strategic market in terms of its geographic location and economic power, offering a low-cost, highly-educated workforce with a work ethic that propelled the country from a virtual wasteland to one of the world's largest economies in just one short generation.

AmCham reminds foreign businesspeople that the cultural aspect of doing business in South Korea takes precedence over virtually all other considerations, and that while South Koreans often make exceptions for foreigners, there are many customs and norms the expatriate businessperson encounters daily that cannot be ignored.

Surprising, perhaps, to newcomers in the field of international business, expatriate managers in South Korea (as in other foreign countries) generally end up having more problems with their head offices than they do in their local business relationships—mostly because head office personnel are unable to appreciate the impera-tives of the South Korean way of doing things, and the need to adapt and compromise.

Despite the Western façade that cloaks all of South Korea, from its people to its cities and factors, the cultural and political history of the Korea peninsula created the basic mindset and behavior of the people. It is necessary to know a great deal about this history to understand and appreciate Koreans and how they do business.

CHAPTER ONE

A Historical Profile

The Korean Peninsula has been inhabited for at least 30,000 years, and perhaps for tens of thousands of years longer. Prior to 1,000 B.C., family clans lived in villages, tilled the fields around them, hunted, and fished. Their religion consisted of shamanism, in which natural objects such as trees, rivers, and rocks were believed to have spirits. (These religious practices survive today in some rural areas.)

Early Kingdoms

Korea's Bronze Age began around 1,000 B.C., lasted for about a thousand years, and was followed by an Iron Age, which ended in approximately A.D. 935. In 350 B.C. the first tribal league, Chosun, centered in northern Korea, was at the apex of its power. Other tribal groups that existed on the Korean Peninsula at that time included the Chinhan, Pyonhan, and Mahan.

In 108 B.C. China sent a large expeditionary force to Korea and established a kind of vassal relationship with the tribal leagues, which soon thereafter coalesced into three competing kingdoms—Silla (57 B.C. to A.D. 935), Paekche (18 B.C. to A.D. 600), and

Koguryo (37 B.C. to A.D. 668). By the first century A.D., the people of the three Korean kingdoms had developed a sophisticated lifestyle based on patterns long established in China. This development continued during the next several centuries, with Buddhism and Confucianism being added to native shamanistic religious practices.

The Korean kingdoms adopted China's social and political systems, dividing the people into classes, with the royal families, elite government administrators, and educators at the top. The Chinese system of writing was also adopted. Those wishing to enter governmental service competed in annual examinations—another import from China.

In A.D. 668 the kingdom of Silla became supreme throughout the peninsula, giving Korea its first golden age. When Silla was at its peak, between A.D. 700 and 800, the capital city of Kyongju had a population of over one million, and was one of the most modern cities in the world. Many of Korea's greatest Buddhist temples were built during this period. This was also the period that saw the rise of unarmed martial arts.

The Silla dynasty gave way to the Koryo dynasty (from which modern Korea takes its name) in A.D. 935. The Koryo king gave Buddhism special status in the country in A.D. 950, resulting in it playing a dominant role in the history of the country until the fall of the dynasty in 1392. Confucianism, which is more of a social system than a religion, also permeated South Korean culture during the Koryo period, and was to have its heyday during the next great dynasty.

The importance of Buddhism and Confucianism, both of which relied on written texts for their propagation, led to Korea's first printing press, which originally used wooden blocks and then began using movable metal type in A.D. 1234—a first in the world. Korea's famed celadon pottery was also developed during this period.

In the latter part of the 1200s, Genghis Khan and his Mongol hordes made Koryo a vassal state of China. King Kojong fled to the island of Kwangha, where he had all the Buddhist scriptures carved on 81,258 wooden blocks, an undertaking that required sixteen years. (The blocks may be seen today at the Haeinsa Mountain Temple.) The Mongol influence in Korea lasted for over one hundred years.

The Last Dynasty

Korea's last dynasty, Choson (also known as Yi), was founded in A.D. 1392, when General Song-Gye Yi (Yi is also written as Lee) seized power. Yi moved the capital to Seoul, its present location.

The Choson government adopted a new, extreme form of Confucianism as the foundation of both the government and society, dividing the people into classes and beginning the process of establishing a system of etiquette and ethics that was to prevail for the next 500 years and create the national character that continues to distinguish South Koreans to this day.

The most famous of the Yi kings was Sejong, who ascended the throne in 1418. An enlightened and progressive ruler, Sejong established schools throughout the country, where learned professors taught political science, history, medicine, geography, and other subjects, including Confucianism.

Sejong is personally credited with making significant technological advances in water clocks, the sundial, rain gauges, and the lunar calendar. He was also responsible for setting up a team of scholars to specifically devise a purely Korean system of writing, called *Hangul* (hahn-guul), for the country's language.

But Sejong's successors continued to expand the influence of the new, extreme form of Confucianism throughout the government and society. In 1471 these neo-Confucian principles were codified in the Great Administration Code and made the law of the land. The law officially established four distinct hereditary social classes. The elite *yangban*, made up of scholars and high ranking military officers, was designated the ruling class. Next came the *joong-in*, made up of professionals (doctors, lawyers, geographers, translators, and middle-ranked military officers). Third in rank were the *sang-min*, which included artisans, craftsmen, fishermen, farmers who were ex-soldiers, and merchants.

The lowest class was made up of servants, butchers, entertainers, *kisaeng* girls, sorcerers, felons, and slaves. The code also decreed that only direct lineal male members of the highest class (the *yangban*) were eligible to take the civil service examinations for government service, which had been held annually since the year A.D. 655. Part of the preparation for the civil service exams was learning some 20,000 Chinese characters (King Sejong's simplified *Hangul* characters didn't count), and mastering the art of calligraphy.

This new Confucian state, which emphasized the past and with few exceptions discouraged change or innovation of any kind, was to keep Korea at a virtual standstill for the next 400 years.

During the more than 500 years of the Choson dynasty, several generations usually lived in a family compound—the men in the front and the women in the back. Boys and girls were separated at the age of seven, at which time boys started school while girls were kept at home, and in lower-class families acted as servants to the male members of the family. When sons married they set up housekeeping in their family compound.

Men were free to come and go as they pleased, but women were virtually slaves. Upper-class women were prohibited from leaving their compounds during the day, and could go out at night for brief periods only with the permission of their husbands. In Seoul, the hour at which the women could leave their homes and go outside was noted by the ringing of a great bell, which also sounded when they were to be back in their homes.

Because of this strictly enforced edict, many women lived all their lives without seeing Seoul during daylight hours. Men could divorce their wives at any time for any one of seven "sins," among which were talking too much, not pleasing their mother-in-laws, and failure to bear sons. This social system prevailed in Korea until well into the twentieth century, and was responsible for fashioning what is now often referred to as the traditional South Korean character.

Contact with Japan

Prior to the establishment of the Choson dynasty, Korea's relations with Japan had mostly been friendly. In fact, Korea, along with China, had been the wellspring for much of Japanese civilization, beginning around A.D. 350. But in the mid-1400s, Japanese pirates began raiding the Korean coastal areas, and thereafter relations between the two countries deteriorated.

In 1592, Japan's Hideyoshi Toyotomi, who had just become the supreme military power in Japan after a long period of clan warfare, sent a huge army to Korea, determined to conquer the peninsula and then proceed on to invade China—apparently to extract revenge from the Chinese for their role in the attempted invasions of Japan by Genghis Khan and his Mongol hordes in 1274 and 1281.

However, the first Japanese invasion ships to approach Korea were defeated by Korea's famed Admiral Sun-Shin Yi, whose iron-clad warships, the world's first, caught the Japanese by surprise. But the large Japanese army of skilled and experienced warriors was not to be denied. They eventually established a beachhead, then began a systematic campaign of laying waste to the country and butchering everyone who opposed them. They sliced the ears off of thousands of their victims, pickled them, and sent them back to Japan as evidence of their success.

The Japanese troops occupied large portions of Korea and settled in for a long campaign. Among those joining the Japanese occupying forces was a Spanish Catholic priest, who began preaching Christianity to Koreans in the conquered areas. He was the first Westerner of record to set foot in Korea.

Before the Japanese army could complete the subjugation of Korea, however, Hideyoshi Toyotomi became ill. Fearful that his newly-established military control of Japan might be threatened, he recalled the army from Korea. He died before they could reach Japan and prevent his fears from becoming a reality.

The death and destruction wrought on Korea by the Japanese discouraged Koreans from having any kind of foreign relations. The country was sealed off to the outside world and became known as "The Hermit Kingdom" for almost three hundred years. Ironically, it was Japan that pried the Hermit Kingdom open and then brought about its downfall.

In 1876 a Japanese ship appeared off the coast of southern Korea and was fired on by shore batteries. When the ship's crew returned to Japan and reported the incident, the highly militant Japanese mounted a crushing attack against the inexperienced and primitively armed Korean defense forces, and once again established a beachhead on Korean soil.

Colonization by Japan

Japan demanded that Korea renounce its isolationist policy and open its ports to Japanese naval and merchant ships (in an almost exact reenactment of their own experiences—minus the invasion—with the United States navy in the 1850s). Six years later, Korea extended the same rights to the U.S., and shortly thereafter to other nations as well.

From this time on, Japan rapidly extended its influence in Korea, resulting in a breakdown of its relations with China and Russia. Following its successful war against China in 1895 and against Russia in 1904–5, Japan began turning Korea into a colony, taking over the government and all major industries.

In 1910 Japan formally ended the Choson dynasty by making Korea a part of the Japanese empire. The Japanese occupation forces immediately began a brutal program aimed at Japanizing the Koreans by outlawing their language and many of their cultural practices, and forcing them to adopt Japanese names.

Japan's control of Korea continued until the end of World War II in 1945, when it was defeated by the U.S. and its allies. Unfortunately, the U.S. agreed to allow Soviet Russia to administer the portion of Korea north of the 38th parallel until a South Korean government could be established to replace the defeated Japanese. The Russians immediately established a Communist regime in northern Korea, thereafter refusing all entreaties to reunite the country.

Elections were held in South Korea in 1948. Syngman Rhee, a patriot who had long been in exile in Hawaii, was elected president. In the meantime, Soviet Russia installed Kim Il-sung, a dedicated Communist who had been indoctrinated in the Soviet Union, as president of North Korea.

In June 1950, after five years of Communist indoctrination, North Korean troops invaded South Korea, believing that the only way to reunite the country was to drive the Americans out of the south.

U.S. and United Nations troops soon pushed the invading North Koreans back to the Yalu River, and the war seemed to be over. China then joined the fighting on the side of North Korea. American and UN forces suffered heavy losses and were driven southward to the vicinity of Busan.

General Douglas MacArthur, supreme commander of the Allied powers occupying Japan at that time, led the American forces in a counterattack through the port of Inchon west of Seoul on the Yellow Sea side of the peninsula. The move outflanked the Chinese and North Koreans and drove them back to the 38th parallel, where the war became a stalemate as a result of a political decision by the American government. A ceasefire was called, and in July 1953 an armistice agreement was signed, establishing a two-kilometer demilitarized zone along the 38th parallel and setting up the framework for peace talks between the North and South.

More than half a century later, the talks were still going on and the country is still divided. Families that were torn apart have not seen each other since 1950. And like the infamous wall in Berlin, the demilitarized zone and the peace-talk site at Panmunjom have become tourist attractions.

The Korean War and Its Aftermath

The Korean War (1950–53) had brought new death and destruction to South Koreans on a massive scale. But the suffering of the South Korean people was not over. The government under Syngman Rhee was rife with corruption and the abuse of power. Student uprisings finally forced Rhee to retire in 1960.

With Rhee gone, Myun J. Chang took over as president, but in May 1961 a bloodless coup led by General Park Chung-hee cut short his administration.

For the next eight years ex-general Park gave South Korea harsh but efficient rule, instituting many reforms and inaugurating the first of a series of five-year plans that were to create an economic miracle. Park was assassinated in October 1979. Choi Kyu-hah served as president for two months, and was replaced on December 12, 1979 by Chun Doo-hwan, under whose strict military-style leadership the economic miracle of the Republic of South Korea continued to unfold.

In early 1987, disenchantment with the militaristic regime of ex-general Chun reached boiling point. University students once again took to the streets, bringing on a series of increasingly violent confrontations with the national police and armed forces. Finally, Roh Tae-woo, newly appointed chairman of the ruling Democratic Justice Party and Chun's hand-picked successor, abruptly capitulated to the demands of the students and the main opposition parties, announcing in late June that the constitution would be revised and a democratic form of government adopted.

It is against this backdrop of shamanism, Buddhism, Confucianism, a strict hierarchal society, and decades of suffering and anguish at the hands of foreign powers, along with internal political strife, that one must view present-day South Korea and its people.

CHAPTER TWO

The Basics of Korean Etiquette & Ethics

In pre-modern Korea, as in all Confucian-oriented cultures, a minutely structured social system and a precisely scripted etiquette took the place of ethics based on principles of right and wrong. Koreans were ethical and moral if they conducted themselves according to the rules of conduct established by the government—rules that were based on sustaining a society that was hierarchically divided by gender and class, and ruled over by an elite upper class.

In this environment, relationships between people were absolutely controlled by the individual's gender and place in the inferior-superior vertically arranged society. There was virtually no social intercourse between classes, and the elite, hereditary upper class reigned supreme over the lower classes.

Koreans also typically ignored those with whom they had no relationship, because to do otherwise would require establishing a connection that resulted in a variety of social obligations. This system dramatically limited the dynamics of South Korean society as a whole, and combined with the Confucian concept of worshipping ancestors and looking back instead of forward, was the reason why the country stagnated, socially, politically, and economically, until its encounters with Japan and the West at the end of the 19th century.

What all this means today insofar as business is concerned is the fact that *kongson* (kohng-sohn), or the South Korean style courtesy, often takes precedence over Western concepts of ethical behavior. And this can be even more disconcerting to Westerners because the courtesy that South Koreans exhibit toward others generally depends upon a number of factors—age, gender, position, social class, and any existing relationship, etc.—instead of being a universal thing.

Fortunately, as far as South Koreans are concerned, foreigners are "cultural free"—meaning they are not bound by the rules of South Korean etiquette and all the obligations involved—so South Koreans have no qualms about meeting and interacting with them, and many, in fact, aggressively seek relationships with foreigners for economic as well as social reasons.

The Perils of Using Logic

It is generally accepted that the foundation of Western thought is based on logical, rational reasoning—although this is not always obvious when you consider the history of the West.

Koreans, on the other hand, were traditionally steeped in Confucian principles that gave precedence to an enforced social harmony that generally ignored both *nolli* (nohl-lee), or logic, and rationality insofar as natural human instincts and aspirations were concerned. Koreans were conditioned to suppress their emotions, to eschew individualistic, independent thinking and behavior, and to scrupulously obey the etiquette and group orientation prescribed by Confucianism and interpreted by their authoritarian governments.

In this environment, the use of logic and rational thinking was taboo, except in special situations created and controlled by the authorities on different levels. Korean sociologist Choe Chae-sok says that the traditional conditioning of Koreans in a formalistic, ritualistic social system made them incapable of rational thought and behavior—a critique that is no longer valid.

Industrialization has its own mandates that demand logical, rational behavior, and the modernization of South Korea has dramatically weakened the hold that Confucianism had on the culture. South Koreans are no longer mired up to their necks in a social system based on non-logic and irrationality, but many have not yet thrown off the influence of centuries of intensive brainwashing that programmed them to regard much of the logic and rational thinking of the West as anti-social.

Westerners who present their arguments and cases to Koreans in a strictly logical manner, with facts, figures and projections, almost always encounter some degree of resistance. In some instances, the resistance may be total.

Still today, many Koreans regard people who always think and behave in a logical manner as disruptive rather than constructive, with extreme cases being looked upon as anti-human.

One of the most common complaints that South Koreans voice about Westerners, Americans in particular, is that their logical stance makes them inflexible and therefore hard to deal with. They also add that American businessmen, diplomats, and politicians talk too much, repeat themselves too often, and little by little weaken their own arguments in an effort to get agreements.

Americans, they add, repeatedly use the terms "fair" and "just" in their arguments and presentations, without being aware that what is fair and just to them is often not perceived as such by others. The challenge, of course, is for foreigners to become familiar enough with South Korean culture that they can combine the two value systems to come up with a workable relationship.

Westerners who are new to South Korea automatically expect South Koreans to react in a logical, or *nollijogin*, manner based on their own cultural experiences. However, this often does not happen, since South Koreans have been culturally conditioned for centuries to react on the basis of personal factors and prevailing circumstances, which may not only be inherently different but changeable. It is therefore necessary to have some knowledge of

South Korean cultural attitudes and behavior before you can predict their reaction to a given setting, since it may not be "logical" in the Western sense.

The Ethics of Group Consciousness

As noted, traditional Korean ethics had their genesis in Confucianism. One of the outgrowths of this Confucian influence was the emotional and intellectual homogenization of Koreans to the point that *chung* (chuung) or "group consciousness" virtually replaced individual awareness.

In order to make *chung* acceptable to the Korean people, the Confucian-dominated Choson court equated group consciousness with morality, and made it the law of the land. Between 1400 and 1900 the concept of group consciousness became so deeply embedded in the psyche of Koreans that it is still visible today—over 100 years after it was discarded as the "official morality" during the last years of the Choson dynasty.

Chung is visible in present-day South Korea within families and in the workplace, but it is no longer the foundation for all South Korean actions. The challenge facing foreign managers in South Korea is to distinguish between the old morality of *chung* and the new morality based on the rights and welfare of the individual in their dealings with employees, suppliers, and customers.

Generally speaking, South Koreans today continue to believe that group consciousness is often superior to the Western cowboy or "go-it-alone" approach to things, and are adamant in their beliefs. *Chung*, which we just translated as "group consciousness," is also the South Korean word for loyalty. But loyalty in the traditional South Korean sense was (and often still is) quite different from what the word means to Westerners.

Again, broadly speaking, loyalty in the Western sense is an ethical position based on an unchanging principle. Loyalty in the traditional South Korean sense can be described as "situational ethics." In other words, what is ethical today may not be ethical tomorrow if the situation changes.

This traditional form of ethics is still very much alive in South Korean culture, because it has proven to be a significant advantage in today's competitive business world. Obviously, this flex-ibility in ethics can be very disturbing to the Western businessper-son who is looking for and expects continuity and predictability in commitments and relationships.

South Koreans are especially sensitive to any sign that their foreign partners are not loyal in the South Korean sense—which means being willing and able to contend with contingencies that may occur regularly, requiring adjustments in commitments and contracts. It is difficult for foreigners without a deep knowledge of South Korean culture to recognize and deal with the various aspects of *chung*. And this is another situation where having an older South Korean on staff or as a consultant is useful, keep-ing both sides on the same cultural channel and accommodating each other.

The "Good Mood" Syndrome

Kibun (kee-boon), which means "feelings" or "mood," is one of the most important facets of South Korean psychology. South Koreans are extraordinarily sensitive to slights and setbacks that damage their *kibun* and upset the harmony of their existence, and they go to what appear to Westerners to be extreme lengths to maintain their own *kibun* as well as that of those around them.

This conditioned cultural reflex influences virtually every nuance of the private as well as public lives of South Koreans, and is part of their institutions of etiquette, politeness, and respect. The *kibun* factor often plays a decisive role in business because South Koreans do not like to give anyone bad news, since such news will obviously damage the recipient's *kibun*. This results in a variety of reactions. Unpleasant news or information may be totally withheld, it may be delayed until near the end of the day to avoid spoiling the person's day, or it may be softened, sometimes to the point that it is misleading.

South Koreans especially dislike being the bearer of unpleasant news to someone who has a hot temper and reacts emotionally—particularly since they also equate class, breeding, and character with keeping one's emotions under control and responding to any situation calmly. But this cultural programming can result in a kind of catch-22 situation because the demands of South Korean etiquette makes them very emotional and subject to reactions that range from subtle to loud outbursts that sometimes turn violent.

In all dealings in South Korea, personal and business, it is important to keep this facet of the South Korean character in mind, and avoid any unnecessary assaults on anyone's *kibun*.

Dealing with Sensitive Feelings

There are a number of refrains that Westerners doing business in South Korea (and elsewhere in Confucian Asia) often hear—almost always when some misunderstanding, dispute, or difference of opinion occurs—which can be a daily occurrence.

The most common of these refrains is: "You must understand the South Korean way!" (or the Chinese way or the Japanese way, depending on where you are). In South Korea the outsider cannot begin to grasp the meaning and implications of "the South Korean way" without an understanding of *kibun* in all of its cultural nuances.

In its full cultural context *kibun* incorporates most of the values South Koreans hold dear. It is the foundation of harmony. It sets the tone, style, and quality of all their relationships. "Face," dignity, pride, respect, and more are bound up in the meaning and role of *kibun*.

For South Koreans to develop and maintain harmonious relationships they must be able to accurately "read" the *kibun* of others, adjust their own expectations and behavior accordingly, and at the same time protect their own feelings.

Richard Saccone says in his book, *The Business of South Korean Culture*, that the goal of *kibun* is to help people stay unthreatened, relaxed, comfortable, and happy. This makes it imperative that people avoid or ignore many situations that are commonplace in business and everyday life, from minor mistakes and embarrassments to very serious matters.

A person's *kibun* can be damaged, resulting in a negative reaction, by many things that usually involve failure to follow the rules of South Korean etiquette. These things include not bowing properly to a superior, failure to use respectful language, not using a person's title, unintentionally treating a senior as a subordinate, giving the wrong kind of gift, being the bearer of bad news, criticizing someone in public, questioning someone's veracity or honesty, and so on.

One or more of these failures invariably results in the individual on the receiving end feeling resentment, developing a grudge, and thereafter looking upon the offender as an enemy.

Kibun jo kye (kee-buun joe-kay) refers to the "face" or "manner" that one presents to others to ensure that they will feel good and friendly—something that is crucial in developing and sustaining good relationships in South Korea.

Dealing with Powerful Emotions

Western businesspeople who go into South Korea without being familiar with the culture are often surprised, and sometimes shocked, at how emotional South Koreans can be, often in situations that would not raise an eyebrow in the West.

The reason for this trait is, of course, an outgrowth of South Korea's traditional Confucian-oriented culture. Until the end of the feudal system in 1910, demonstrations of *kamdong* (kahm-dohng), or emotion, were virtually taboo. Among the few exceptions were demonstrations of affection and love for young children.

Confucianism looked upon love and other expressions of emotion as disruptive to society, and mandated a social system in which emotions were suppressed in the interest of a perfectly harmonious family, community, and country.

Of course, this enforced repression of the emotions resulted in the build-up of frustrations and friction that frequently erupted in some kind of violence. But this reaction was rare enough in public that the South Korean reputation for being calm and peaceful remained intact.

Now that the system of official sanctions that kept the lid on the emotions of South Koreans for so many generations have been eliminated and the social sanctions have weakened considerably, expressions of *kamdong*—both positive and the negative—are commonplace.

Some of the emotional outbursts of present-day South Koreans are collective in nature, and involve such things as strikes and other kinds of demonstrations. Others outbursts are personal and often domestic, primarily between husbands and wives.

In business situations, *kamdong* generally manifests itself in covert actions against specific individuals within companies. Employees who feel that they have been shamed or wronged in any way will generally not complain openly, but will take some kind of action to punish the offenders.

Identifying disgruntled employees is not always easy, as they can be clever at disguising their feelings. This calls for very sensitive attention being paid to the mix of employees—age, sex, education, birthplace, etc.—plus having at least one or more loyal and supportive employees who are tuned into what is going on in an office or workshop and will advise the manager when there is a problem and how to resolve it.

Avoiding the Appearance of Arrogance

Koman (koh-mahn), or arrogance, is one of the many common human traits that was made taboo by Korea's Confucian-based government. The edicts applying to *koman* covered those in elite positions, including the king, and the higher a person's social position who behaved in an arrogant manner, the greater the sin.

Of course, this does not mean that arrogance was eliminated from Korean society. The power that the social system gave to officials and fathers was such that it bred arrogance in many men, but blatant examples of arrogance were, in fact, relatively rare, and in extreme cases were fatal to officials who went beyond what people could endure.

The social sanctions against arrogance are not as draconian as they were in feudal Korea, but South Koreans remain especially sensitive to arrogant behavior. And as it happens, some of the typical behavior of Westerners seems arrogant to South Korean eyes. This behavior includes bragging, criticizing others, being aggressive in manner and presentations, and making disparaging comments about anything Korean. The mere fact that a foreign manager insists on something being done exactly as he orders can be taken as arrogance if it implies that the employee concerned would otherwise not be capable of doing it.

But today, arrogant posturing and arrogant behavior in South Korea is not limited to foreigners who have not learned how to function in a cross-cultural setting. Extraordinary economic success by South Korea has resulted in some South Koreans in both industry and government letting their success go to their heads and their arrogance can be palpable.

Dealing with South Korean Nationalism

The etiquette and ethics that South Koreans display in their relationships with foreign businesspeople and others invariably have a strong flavoring of *kukkajuui* (kuuk-kah-juu-we) or "nationalism."

South Korea has a 5,000-year history that is marked by numerous invasions by its neighbors, and two attempts by the Japanese to totally destroy its indigenous culture. The last invasion of the country by Japan, at the beginning of the 20th century, was aimed at eliminating both the culture and Korea as a nation.

But the Koreans survived all of these depredations, and became all the more independent minded and strong-willed because of their suffering. Their pride in themselves and in their country is unbounded.

South Koreans regard themselves as a unique people, and take great pride in using the phrase *Uri Hanguksaram* (Uh-ree-Hahn-guuk-sah-rahm), which means "We Koreans," and is a ringing pronouncement that has racial, cultural, social, geographic, economic, and political implications.

South Koreans take great pride in the now generally acknowledged fact that it was Korean immigrants who founded Japan's first recorded Imperial Court, and that virtually all of the arts and crafts for which Japan is now famous were introduced into Japan by Koreans.

These historical facts help explain the strong nationalism of South Koreans, but not the extreme nationalism of North Koreans, which is an aberration that cannot be explained in rational terms.

The extraordinary *kukkajuui* of South Koreans has played a vital role in the economic success of the country, manifesting itself in the energy and ambitions of the people as well as in government policies that have been designed to benefit the nation, often at the expense of its trading partners.

New government policies adopted at the beginning of the 21st century are designed to promote further economic growth, turning the country into a high-tech and cultural hub in East Asia. And while the nationalism exhibited by government agencies and individuals may sometimes result in handicaps for foreign businesspeople, the desire of the South Koreans to continue building on their success is so strong that the windows of opportunity for foreign companies in South Korea are greater than ever.

It is, however, vitally important for foreign businesspeople to understand the sources of the nationalism of the people of South Korea, and deal with it diplomatically.

The Western Way vs. the South Korean Way

Historically, Europeans and Americans have taken the position that they can do business with anyone, even with strangers they have never met and may never meet.

In pre-modern Korea, on the other hand, all relationships, social, business, and otherwise, were based on prior relationships resulting from family ties, community, school, and work. Any kind of relationship outside of one's family or circle of close relatives carried with it a special set of obligations that could range from bothersome and expensive to dangerous. This factor resulted in Koreans limiting the number of relationships they had in both their private and public lives.

This facet of traditional Korean culture has weakened considerably since the last decades of the 20th century, but it is still a significant factor in the lives of most South Koreans, especially the older generation.

Foreigners in South Korea generally have a special advantage because they can ignore many of the more subtle obligations involved in meeting and establishing relationships with new people. And they can avoid this because South Koreans do not automatically expect them to behave like Koreans. But totally ignoring the Korean way in establishing and maintaining business as well as social relationships can be dangerous, and may result in a variety of unpleasant repercussions, as Koreans are culturally conditioned to seek redress, if not outright revenge, for behavior considered unethical or immoral—meaning un-Korean.

What is Fair in South Korea?

The ethical and philosophical concept of *kongpyong* (kohng-p'yong), or fairness, did not exist in feudal Korea in the Western sense. The Confucian social system that prevailed was based on precise hierarchical relationships between inferiors and superiors, and between classes. Confucian ideology did not recognize the principle of equality.

Koreans' early attitudes to fairness and equality in human relationships, business, and professional affairs did not develop until the introduction of democracy and other Western principles into South Korea in the 20th century. Prior to this, inequality was the norm.

Social class, political power, and wealth no longer have absolute, government-sanctioned priority over human rights and fairness, but *kongpyong* still has a traditional slant in the context of Korean business and politics.

Fairness as a fundamental principle of human rights and behavior has experienced the most acceptance and growth in family and personal relationships. The younger the age level of individuals, the more they have become committed to the principle of fairness in all of their relationships.

In business etiquette and ethics, the level or degree of *kongpyong* in the Western sense varies with the age and size of the company, the age and background of the ranking managers and executives, whether it is domestic or internationally oriented, and so on. With the variable exception of individuals who have been educated in the West and/or spent enough years there to absorb the nuances of fairness and equality in their Western context, it is still normal for South Koreans to interpret *kongpyong* with a Korean flavor.

This means that foreigners doing business in South Korea must be sensitive to the possible variations in the understanding and application of fairness, keeping in mind that Koreans generally view the concept from their own cultural, social, economic, and national perspective. In other words, their fairness may not be a fundamental stand-alone principle that is, or can be, applied universally to any situation.

One of the attitudes of smaller businesspeople in South Korea is the notion that they should not be held to the same standards as large companies in their dealings, a viewpoint that they regard as ethically fair. On a more basic level, South Koreans as a whole do not believe it is fair, or morally right, for the United States and other larger, richer countries, to demand equal trade rights with South Korea.

Since the concept of fairness in South Korea is subject to a variety of interpretations, foreign businesspeople—who are generally steeped in the idea of fairness as a universal concept—must be prepared to resolve any issues that arise by either accommodating their Korean counterparts or winning them over.

The Emotional Content of Business

Western businesspeople should be aware of, and keep in mind, the role that feelings play in Korean behavior. Their emotions are just below the surface and can be turned on with startling suddenness over something that the outsider might not regard as important.

Behavioral scientists in South Korea say this penchant for extreme emotional behavior is a result of the fact that historically, there was no socially acceptable way for differences of opinion and disputes to be settled through rational discussion and debate.

If a wife wanted to get her husband's attention she had to scream and throw a tantrum. When men wanted to make a point they got drunk and started a fight. If workers wanted to express their displeasure about something, they went out on a strike that often became violent—but in a controlled, structured way.

This tendency to be emotionally volatile is still a part of the character of Koreans, and is generally kept under control by the use of polite and/or laudatory language, and by being especially careful not to do or say anything that others would find offensive.

Another factor in interpersonal relationships in South Korea is the use of feelings to persuade, motivate, and otherwise manipulate people—rather than using logic and proof to win them over.

This factor is often a major stumbling block for the typical Westerner, whose approach in business and social situations is generally to use facts and a rational presentation to bring someone around.

Koreans, especially Korean women, are aware of the Western weakness when it comes to dealing with loud, emotional outbursts, and have been known to make use of it to carry the day.

CHAPTER THREE

The Enduring Korean Character

Outwardly, South Korea today is nothing at all like it was in the 1950s or 1960s, or even 1970s, and yet its underlying principles of society and business have changed very little. Liberation from Japanese rule in 1945 and from American dominance in the 1950s was followed by the rapid introduction of a Western facade that has changed the appearance of its cities and its countryside.

Most South Koreans have been partially de-Koreanized by years of exposure to and involvement with Westerners, particularly Americans, and hundreds of thousands have been educated abroad and are now either bicultural, or at least bilingual, and able to function in both South Korean and Western environments.

The family is still of vital importance. There is still respect for authority, the aged, and the learned. South Korean society is still generally organized on an intricate network of personal connections; an authoritarian hierarchy in corporations persists and people still adopt face-saving facades, emphasizing class and rank.

Modern-day South Korea is a work in progress and is becoming more and more modern but within the remnants of one of the most traditional, comprehensive cultures the world has ever seen. It is therefore necessary to know a great deal about the traditional culture of Koreans.

Humanism and Benevolence in Business

Another interesting and important facet of South Korean ethics is their traditional commitment to humanistic acts of benevolence—something that probably grew out of their historical experience of living under regimes in which life was hard, and helping each other was often a matter of survival.

Another aspect of benevolent acts by Korea's ruling class during feudal times was no doubt influenced by the "largess of the lord"—when they would, on certain occasions, bestow gifts and other kinds of favors on common people.

In any event, the kind of humanism that results in benevolent behavior was characteristic of common people during the country's long feudal history, and South Korean sociologists say that the core character of the people was subsumed in the word *in* (een), which can be translated as both humanism and benevolence, and they add that the term incorporates the concepts of kindness, meekness, and wisdom.

In present-day South Korea this ancient interpretation of humanism is reflected in attitudes toward the government and toward employers—the idea being that what they say and do should be guided by humanistic principles.

The rationale that all work-related situations should conform to the Korean view of humanistic behavior has a direct impact on all labor relations in South Korea, and is something that foreign employers should be aware of in managing their South Korean-based companies or offices.

Defining South Korean Management

South Korean social science professors and other scholarly types often say there is no such thing as Korean-style management (*kwalli*), then go on to describe a system that is typically Korean. What they apparently mean is that there is not one uniform style of management in South Korea, but a number of "styles" that differ to varying degrees, being mixtures of Korean and Western approaches, along with features that reflect the individual philosophies and experiences of their founders or leaders.

The industrial revolution did not get underway in Korean until the Japanese invaded and annexed the country in 1910. The companies set up by the Japanese in Korea, as well as those founded by Korean entrepreneurs, were patterned after those that had been established in Japan from the 1870s onwards, and were managed like Confucian family fiefs.

It was not until the 1960s and 1970s that South Korean businessmen began to import and apply Western management practices. Company founders also began sending their sons to business schools in the U.S. and Europe, and by the 1980s these foreign-educated offspring began showing up in South Korean corporations.

But despite the presence of thousands of foreign educated managers and executives in South Korean companies, and the continuing import of Western management technology, South Korean *kwalli* (kwah-lee), or management, continues to be primarily Korean in essence and in flavor.

The structure of South Korean companies is still vertical. Management is a combination of top-down and middle management-up, with fewer documents than is common in Japan and the U.S. Training and discipline are strict. There is virtually no horseplay or joking by employees. Most confrontations and disagreements are settled by edicts from higher up. The emotional content in South Korean *kwalli* is high. Corporations are paternalistic.

Promotions and survival on the managerial level is based on survival of the fittest, and competition is fierce. Relationships— school ties, blood ties, birthplaces, etc.—play important roles in the politics of South Korean companies. Company events and the travels of senior executives are planned and executed with military thoroughness and precision.

South Korean *kwalli* emphasizes sincerity, a serious manner at all times, striving for perfection, absolute loyalty and a willingness to sacrifice for the company, pride in the company and its work. Many major companies run training programs aimed at breaking down the mindset that new recruits bring with them, and reprogramming them to think and behave as a company person with a soldier-like spirit.

Managers are charged with the responsibility of training their subordinates in the philosophy of the corporation, in the attitude and behavior that is expected of them, and in providing them with a variety of incentives to conform and produce. Meetings, speeches, and lectures are frequent.

Foreign companies that set up operations in South Korea must be aware of and conform to many of the management procedures that are expected—and often required by law. This means having input from a variety of Korean sources, including consultants on the cultural aspect of management in South Korea.

Much of the dynamism of the South Korean economy during the 1960s, 1970s, and 1980s came from the extraordinary spirit, dedication, and drive of the founding fathers of many of the country's business enterprises, most of which date from the 1950s and 1960s. They had in common a will to succeed, a missionary zeal, and a self-sacrificing dedication that went far beyond the standards of the typically aggressive businessman. They were able to instil much of this same drive and dedication in the executives and labor force they built up to achieve their goals.

These zealous founders did not rely solely on the benefits of the Confucian ideals of loyalty and work ethic, however. They also applied a vigorous Korean version of the "carrot and stick" or, as it is known in Korean, the *Shin sang pil bol* form of personnel management, which emphasises recognition and incentive and "reward and punishment." Winners were pampered and rewarded, while poor performers were subject to harsh disciplinary action.

With the transition from the founders to the second generation of managers, South Korean companies began to rely on more traditional approaches, including a corporate paternalism that is especially designed to fit the Korean environment. Bonuses, for example, are paid at *kimchi*-making time, *Chusok* (Obon Festival), on the occasion of a death in a family, or when school fees have to be paid.

Because of the group orientation of Korean society, South Korean companies often apply rewards as well as punishments on a group basis. This has the effect of further forging bonds among the groups, which in turn contributes to closer personal ties and cohesiveness among employees, resulting in greater productivity.

"Scold Management"

In a society in which criticism and harsh language of any kind has long been one of the strongest taboos, it is something of a surprise to learn that some larger South Korean companies use severe scolding and criticism at group meetings as a management technique.

These weekly institutionalized meetings, known as *puseo jang hoe* (puh-say-oh jahng hoh-eh), are conducted by senior managers and/or directors and might be termed pep talks—but they are the kind of talks that a loud, brash football coach might give to his under-performing players at half-time.

While the frankness and vehemence of the "scold meetings" vary with the personality of the managers conducting them, they are invariably harsh, even to Western ears.

The rationale is that the manager is acting as a father figure who is doing his duty to berate his children for failing to perform as diligently and as effectively as they should. And the harsher the criticism at a particular meeting, the more likely the same manager or director is to later invite the employees out for a drinking party, as a loving father would do.

Again, this is recognized and acceptable behavior in a strictly Korean setting, but it is not an approach that foreigner managers in South Korea should use. Koreans will take such criticism from their own, but not from others.

Another important phrase in the management vocabulary of Koreans is *tongchal yuk* (tong-chal yahk), or "keen insight," a quality top South Korean businessmen look for in managers being considered for higher executive positions. The individual with this kind of insight is one who has a conspicuously high level of intuitive intelligence and can be expected to make the right decisions most of the time.

Mind Control

Westerners may be put off by any suggestion regarding mind-control, but this wariness is not warranted in the Korean context of controlling the mind. It does not refer to an insidious or evil thing in South Korean culture.

The Korean concept of gaining control of the mind and disciplining it to achieve goals is subsumed in the word *kyong* (k'yohng), which means something like "humble respect for mind control and the development of reason"—concepts that are both Buddhist and Confucian.

Especially from A.D. 1392 until modern times, Koreans were under very serious social and political pressure to control their emotions and their behavior—the latter in line with precise rules of etiquette that covered virtually every aspect of their daily lives.

The cultural programming for this mind-control became an integral part of Korean culture and was learned from infancy onwards, both by osmosis and by direct teaching. While the cultural programming of present-day South Koreans is far less strenuous and comprehensive than during the long feudal era, it is still a major factor in the upbringing, schooling, and corporate training that most South Koreans undergo.

The influence of *kyong* training remains conspicuously visible in the attitudes and behavior of most South Korean employees, managers, and executives, who approach their work and goals with extraordinary focus, diligence, and perseverance.

The *kyong* concept is one of the sources of the "can do (anything)" attitude that is typical of South Koreans—a characteristic that played a leading role in tiny South Korea becoming a major industrial power in a single generation.

Foreign businesspeople in South Korea soon find that Korean-style *kyong* can be a very positive factor in their relationships with employees, suppliers, and others.

Striving for Power

Koreans have always equated *kyoyuk* (k'yoh-yuuk), or education, with power, and with the end of the feudal social system that generally limited learning to the elite upper classes, they have pursued education with obsessive resolve. The resolve to learn extends beyond the school stage, and is pursued as relentlessly by business-people and professionals throughout their working lives because life in South Korea is extraordinarily competitive and because South Koreans view themselves as competing with the rest of Asia and the world at large.

In the 1990s South Korean sociologist Kim Jae-un referred to the South Korean obsession with education as a means of elevating their social status as "diploma disease." He said that much of this feeling was a holdover from the Choson dynasty, during which the ruling class heaped humiliation and degradation on the uneducated lower class.

The Battle for an Education

There is fierce competition in South Korea for entry into the best high schools and universities. Virtually all students in the country take the examinations for Seoul National University (SNU), because it is the most prestigious university and a diploma is practically a guarantee of a desirable career in government or business. Unlike Japan's prestigious Tokyo University, which is private, SNU is a government-run school.

Students who fail in their efforts to enter SNU take the results of the examinations to other prominent universities in declining order of their ranking, hoping to at least get into one of them. Most of those who fail to get into any university end up settling for one of the junior colleges. The most prestigious high school in the country, Kyung Ki, has been in existence for generations. The most elite of the women's colleges is Ehwa (which is sometimes described as the only "real" university for women in South Korea).

Just as it has been for the last thousand years, education and schools are of vital importance in establishing the social status of South Koreans and determining their careers thereafter. The ties that are established during high school and college last throughout life and become the network by which individuals conduct most of their private and professional affairs. People constantly scan the newspapers and other media for the names of classmates and alumni as possible business or personal contacts.

The competitive spirit that drives South Koreans to get an education is directly reflected in their etiquette and ethics in business, and therefore impacts on foreigners doing business in South Korea. Most South Koreans in the business world are far more familiar with Western countries—their history, economics, politics, and culture—than Westerners are with South Korea, and this gives them an advantage in dealing with the typical American or European—not to mention the feelings of cultural superiority that may derive from this circumstance.

Suffice to say that foreigners who undertake the challenge of doing business in South Korea should make a serious point of boning up on Korean history as a key part of their initial preparations.

Etiquette as Morality

We have already commented on the fact that for generations morality in Korea was deeply influenced by Confucian concepts of the structure of an ideal society and how to administer it through carefully prescribed rules of *yeui pomjol* (yeh-we pohm-johl), or etiquette.

This morality based on social etiquette became even more pronounced in 1392, when the newly-established Choson dynasty adopted a far more comprehensive form of Confucianism and made it the foundation of both the government and society at large, and thereafter enforced it by law. When the first Westerners visited Korea they were amazed at the stylish etiquette and dignified behavior of Koreans, but they were also astounded that morality in the Western sense did not seem to exist.

Behavior in present-day South Korea is based on a combination of Western morality and traditional etiquette, which can be confusing to Westerners who like their morality logical, rational, clear-cut, fair, and equally applied to all.

The etiquette-as-morality approach that prevailed in Korea for centuries is fading away, and while foreign businesspeople should abide by the rational courtesies of today's South Korea, they should not compromise on moral and ethical issues based on sound principles of personal and business behavior.

South Koreans continue to be very formal in their meetings

and receptions, particularly higher-ranking government officials and businessmen. Their treatment of Westerners also tends to be quite formal. They are especially respectful toward experienced businessmen and technical professionals, regarding them as teachers in the highest sense.

Like their Japanese neighbors and culturally close kinsmen, the only time South Korean businessmen and government officials dispense with formality is when they are out on the town in informal situations, where drinking is the order of the day.

Dealing with Duty and Obligations

Two of the foundations of Korea's traditional culture were the concepts of *uimu* (we-muu), or duty, and *uiri* (wee-ree), or obligations, which were closely related and often overlapped.

Uimu covered the duty of children to parents, of individuals to their families, of inferiors to superiors, of people to the government, and of the living to the dead.

These duties were emotional, spiritual and intellectual in nature, and became such an integral part of the mindset of the people that they became a national trait. The duties subsumed under *uimu* took precedence over all personal feelings, including love, as well as all other personal considerations or aspirations.

Uiri, or obligation, differed from *uimu* in that it was extrapolated to include the concepts of absolute integrity, loyalty, and the highest standards of Confucian morality, with the goal being to maintain perfect social harmony.

More comprehensive than *uimu*, *uiri* covered the loyalty that parents and children owed to each other and to their kin and friends, to elders, to their teachers, employers, and government officials. People were born with *uiri*, and like original sin in the Christian faith, it stayed with one for life. *Uiri* encompassed all of the etiquette of interpersonal relationships of the living as well as of one's ancestors.

Uimu and *uiri*, combined with collective responsibility, defined Korean society for nearly 500 years, and the legacy of these two concepts continues to influence the behavior of most South Koreans to some degree. While the introduction of democracy and Western-style capitalism into South Korea have significantly reduced the role and power of *uimu* and *uiri*, both are apparent in the attitudes and behavior of the majority of South Koreans.

Where doing business with foreigners are concerned, it continues to be the goal of most South Koreans to create and maintain *uiri*-based relationships, with the emphasis on harmony, loyalty, and integrity.

There are, however, exceptions to this rule: Individuals, and small companies headed by individuals, who do not adhere to the ethics of *uimu* and *uiri* in their dealings with foreigners—and are charlatans in any language.

Korean-Style Sin

Westerners who do business in South Korea should be forewarned that South Korean behavior cannot always be judged on the basis of Western concepts of what is right and wrong—especially things that Westerners tend to think of as "sins" in a spiritual sense.

"Spiritual sin" is primarily a Christian concept, and application of the concept to human behavior is limited to that small portion of humanity that has been indoctrinated in Christian morality.

Koreans have, of course, always had a concept of *choe* (choh-eh), which is usually translated as "sin," but *choe*, as influenced by Confucianism, has been more concerned with conforming to the established etiquette than with spiritual matters or keeping the soul pure. It was more secular than religious.

Anything that upset the hierarchical structure of society and the harmony between the people and the state was regarded as a *choe*. Morality and sin were circumstantial things; not absolute values or principles.

Many South Koreans now accept to some degree the Western concept of sin and morality, especially in male-female relations (because in the Western concept men and women are ostensibly equal), and there are large numbers of South Koreans on every level of industry and government who conduct themselves according to Western morality.

But like the Japanese, most South Koreans are not religious in the Western sense. (This said, a significant percentage of South

Koreans are, in fact, practicing Christians as a result of mission-ary activity in the country beginning in the late 1800s. Korean women in particular were powerfully drawn to the modern Christian concept that women have human rights and should not be isolated and forced to serve men.)

Choe is not related to what happens to the spirit or soul after death. It is what happens in this world that damages individuals, families, friends, or society at large.

Generally speaking, all Koreans, businesspeople, politicians, and all, base their actions not on what is right or wrong from an absolute moral sense, but on what will contribute most to their safety, welfare and success—a criteria that is often much more humane, and more practical, than Christian precepts.

The Personal Nature of Business

In South Korea, as in many other Asian countries, business is a personal affair. The product, profits, and everything else take a backseat to personal relations. If you do not or cannot establish good personal relations with a large network of people, it is either difficult or impossible to do business in South Korea. Personal relations and contacts, combined with a high sense of honor and trust, are the primary foundations of Korean business ethics. Until recent decades written contracts were rare. Most business arrangements were based on verbal agreements.

As a result of this system, South Koreans spend a significant amount of time expanding and nurturing their personal relations because their business depends on it.

The foreign businessman wanting to succeed in South Korea must adapt to this system to a substantial degree. It is essential that the foreign businessman schedule this kind of activity (and expenditure) into the time frame of his plans and expectations. The more you try to rush a decision or activity, particularly before the correct personal relationships have been established, the slower the process will be and the greater the likelihood that your efforts will fail.

"Many foreign businessmen believe that with the right product and price they can easily sell to or buy from any South Korean company. This may be the case in Los Angeles or Hamburg but it doesn't always hold true in South Korea," said Jon Saddoris, president of METEC, a business consultant firm in Seoul.

"Generally speaking, you are not going to get anywhere in South Korea until you establish the necessary 'human relations'," Saddoris adds. This includes approaching the company in the "correct manner," meaning through an acceptable introduction, and on the appropriate level.

Saddoris says that the first mistake many foreign businessmen make in their approach to doing business in South Korea is to believe that meeting the president of a company and getting his approval and cooperation means smooth sailing from then on. In most cases, the managers—lower, middle, and upper—who actually run the company will resent being bypassed and will be less than cooperative, sometimes to the extent that the foreign proposal never gets off the ground floor.

If you have an introduction to the president, it is alright to meet him but you must also meet and establish a satisfactory relationship with the various managers, treating them with the same respect and concern that you extend to the president. This also applies to companies that are still in the hands of founders who appear to make all of the decisions.

In qualifying a South Korean company it is essential that you determine the personal relationships between managers on all levels, especially the relationship between individual managers and directors or the president. Personal ties such as kinship, the same school, the same birthplace, or marriage often take precedence over job seniority, rank, or other factors, and may have a significant influence on who actually runs a company and how it is run. A clear understanding of these ties is often necessary to determine who the real decision-maker is in a South Korean company.

Because personal relations are so important in doing business with South Korean companies, it is vital that you keep up to date on personnel and personal changes within any company concerned. The character and personality of a South Korean company is as changeable as the ties and emotions of the people who make up the organization. It is therefore necessary to treat the relationship as a personal one, requiring regular maintenance.

Although South Koreans now readily sign contracts with foreign companies, the contracts are invariably interpreted personally rather than in the legal sense, and generally speaking are no better than the personal relationship that exists between the two parties. If the relationship is not constantly renewed and reinforced, the contract becomes just a piece of paper.

It is therefore very important for the foreign businessman going into business in South Korea to be personally involved in the process of setting up the operation—along with obtaining the aid and advice of an experienced South Korean to help him make his way through the intricate maze of connections and relationships that are involved.

Once an operation is established, the need for good, solid personal relations becomes more important, rather than diminishes. This means, of course, that the foreign party cannot sit back and relax, as is so often the tendency. The Western habit of relying on contracts and lawyers does not always work in the South Korean environment.

Another aspect of the personal approach to business in South Korea that often upsets Westerners is the tendency for Koreans to run a company as an extension of a large family, which means they make many decisions that are based on purely personal considerations. Koreans are not likely to significantly change this system any time soon, so the only recourse for Westerners is to learn how to cope with it.

The same personal approach necessary for the smooth functioning of an office or company also applies to a corporation's relations with government officials and bureaucrats. Most companies in South Korea assign a particular individual to handle their government relations—invariably the senior member of the company who has the most experience in the bureaucratic arena, and "face" with key government officials.

Government bureaucrats in South Korea are perhaps even more sensitive to the social and business status of people who approach them, and it is especially important for the foreign company having to deal with them to be aware of this. Sending in a young, low-status person is definitely not the way to progress.

More Personal Elements in Business

Americans pride themselves on separating their private and work lives—leaving their work at the factory or office, so to speak. Business in this context is kept as free of personal and emotional considerations as possible.

In Korea businesses have traditionally been run as large extended families with little or no separation between work behavior and personal behavior. Throughout the country's long feudal period the whole of society was based on what Korean sociologists have labeled *sajokuro* (sah-johk-ur-roh) and *yonjul* (yohn-juul), or "personalism" and "connections."

Business in present-day South Korea still has a highly charged personal element, and connections are still the life-line of individual businesspeople as well as corporations. People develop and nurture connections all their lives, and use them as key assets. Business management is first and foremost an exercise in harmonizing and directing the emotional makeup of employees. Every business relationship also has a personal-emotional element that plays a leading role in every aspect of its existence.

Foreigners dealing with South Koreans must be prepared to make a major emotional investment in establishing and maintaining the kind of emotion-rich relationships that are necessary for success. One might say that the whole of Korean etiquette and ethics is based on conforming to, or satisfying, the emotional needs first, and the economic needs second.

Another factor that plays a role in the personalized etiquette and ethics of South Koreans is little or no recognition of the concept of privacy and confidentiality. It is therefore difficult to keep secrets in a South Korean organization. Among other things, it is therefore very important for foreign managers and executives to make sure their personal or private secretaries understand the principle of confidentiality, accept it, and will protect it. Westerners who are ill-at-ease with business relationships that start out on a personal and emotional level, and generally get more intense as time passes, may not be the best managerial candidates for enterprises in South Korea.

Still, today it is often said that one cannot understand Koreans, and function effectively in South Korea without having a good grasp of *in'gan kwan'gye* (een-gahn kwahn-gay), which translates as "interpersonal relationships" and is one of the key phrases used to explain the structure of Korean society and how it works.

While the over-reaching goal of Confucianism was to structure society in such a way that it ensured harmony, the very rules that were designed to control human behavior subverted so many of the natural instincts and aspirations of the people that it simultaneously resulted in deep-seated frustrations that created friction and the potential for disharmony.

In addition to depriving Koreans of the opportunity to think and act as individuals, this system also suppressed virtually all creativity and innovation, and thus kept Korea in a kind of time warp where nothing changed for many generations.

Although a democratic form of government and a free-market economy have released South Koreans from the stagnating aspects of Confucianism, the etiquette and ethics that sustained the old system for some 2,000 years became so deeply embedded in the Korean psyche that they remain a significant part of the national character.

In earlier times, individuals who failed to follow the prescribed national etiquette were regarded as "non-persons." These were almost always people that were of the lowest social order—entertainers, prostitutes, criminals, and foreigners. (Foreigners were added to the list because most of the early foreign visitors were mainly uneducated, unruly sailors, who acted like barbarians when compared to the dignified and formal behavior of Koreans.)

South Koreans are still very class and behavior conscious, but generally there is little if any discrimination against foreigners in general. When South Korean-foreign relationships are concerned, however, particularly in business, foreigners are expected to know and abide by the ethical guidelines that prevail in South Korean society.

Younger South Koreans, less conditioned in the ancient Confucian precepts, are not as well-versed in all of the intricacies of behaving in the traditional Korean way, and they typically ignore many of the old rules and customs while in school. But once they enter the working world, either in private industry or government service, they are required to quickly conform to both the corporate and social culture that prevails in the organization.

One of the facets of contemporary South Korean culture—a holdover from the past—is acute sensitivity to arrogant behavior, or anything that smacks of arrogance. One of the primary principles of Confucianism is the value and importance of humble behavior—from the king or president down to the lowest peasant.

Behaving in a manner that South Koreans perceive as arrogant can result in serious repercussions that are generally covert. Unusually skilled and experienced people can demonstrate their abilities on the job, quietly and unobtrusively, but if they make a big show and/or brag about them, they become pariahs.

Respect in South Korea

Paying respect to parents, elders and others of note in South Korea comes under the heading of *jeol* (juhl), and is still prominent enough in the culture that it can be accurately described as a national trait. This respect takes several different forms and applies to many different occasions, in the use of honorific speech, in bowing, in a deferential manner, in seating arrangements, in who starts to eat first, in gift-giving, etc.

Foreigners in South Korea are given some leeway in conforming to the dictates of *jeol*, but it is both polite and wise to learn enough about South Korean values and customs to demonstrate respect for the people and their culture. From the viewpoint of good business relationships, it is wise because it helps negate the stereotype of Westerners being insensitive to other cultures and arrogant in their behavior.

Besides the business rewards that may accrue from knowing and abiding by *jeol* customs, there is also a personal element. It adds a great deal to the ambiance of living and working in South Korea when you can fit in and feel at home.

Business success for foreigners in South Korea is closely tied to learning and using the respect factor in Korean culture. As with most other key facets of Korean culture, South Korean style *chongyong* (chohn-gyohng), or "paying proper respect," is based on the ideal society promoted by Confucius, which was designed to instill and ensure personal as well as social harmony, and which in turn was based on the suppression of individual interests and desires, and obedience to superiors and authorities.

Until the downfall of feudal Korea, failure to pay the prescribed respect to parents, superiors, and government officials was a very serious breach of both etiquette and the law, and in worse-case scenarios could have disastrous results for individuals and families.

On a personal basis, modern-day South Koreans are generally respectful to their parents and other elders by choice, in a formal as well as an informal sense. But in schools and in workplaces the demands of *chongyong* remain quite strong.

Individuals are normally excruciatingly diligent in paying special respect to their bosses and other seniors, in both their behavior and the language they use. And just as important, South Koreans who have not been de-Koreanized by Western influence are acutely sensitive about other people paying them the respect that they believe is due their position, age, sex, education, and experience.

Where foreigners are concerned, there is a decided nationalistic flavor to the respect that South Koreans expect. Pride in country, pride in their ancient and recent accomplishments, runs deep in Koreans, and any perceived slight is likely to get an emotional response that may be overt or covert, depending on the situation.

Broadly speaking, foreigners in South Korea, businesspeople and others, must go a bit beyond Western ideas of respect in dealing with employees and government officials in order to avoid ruffling the very sensitive feathers of South Koreans.

The Personal Loyalty Factor
As already noted, personal relationships and a minutely prescribed etiquette within social classes defined and controlled virtually all

behavior in feudal Korea. This system worked only because an extreme standard of *songshilham* (sohng-sheel-hahm), or loyalty, was imposed on the people, beginning with the family and going on up to the community and clan.

In its Korean context loyalty was equated with upholding all of the rules and customs controlling the behavior of individuals and groups, and required suppressing all independent thinking and individualistic behavior.

In this environment, loyalty was a personalized thing that depended upon circumstances, not something based on principles, and could therefore change as circumstances changed.

While the feudal family and class system that prevailed in Korea until the middle of the 20th century have undergone dramatic changes, most South Koreans today still view and practice loyalty as a personal thing, not as something required by ethics or morality.

In business and politics in South Korea today, personalized loyalty—to family and classmates in particular—continues to be a major influence that often takes precedence over experience and talent. Expressed another way, South Korean-style loyalty frequently takes precedence over logical and rational thinking.

Foreign businesspeople—and diplomats—working in South Korea should keep in mind that the emotional content of loyalty generally overrides the logical content. The loyalty of South Korean employees often appears to be as much to individual managers and executives as to companies.

Saving Everybody's Face
Korea was still a deeply Confucian society when World War II ended in 1945, and South Koreans did not really began to slough off centuries of social restraints until the 1960s, and even then it was generally only the very young who began, little by little, to ignore deeply entrenched social attitudes and behavior.

For more than 500 years the people of Korea had lived in a social system that made a carefully prescribed etiquette the foundation for the national morality—a foundation that was based on sex, age, social class, and official position, and conditioned people to be obsessed with making sure that others treated them with an exaggerated level of formal courtesy and respect.

In this system, people became so sensitive to the attitudes and behavior of others that *chae-myun* (chay-me'yun) or face-saving, became one of their highest priorities and took up a great deal of their time and energy.

This face-saving syndrome incorporated not only the individual, but the individual's family, and often took precedence over rationality, practicality, and the truth. The need for *chae-myun* was so powerful that it influenced every aspect of behavior, especially how language was used.

In this environment, speaking directly and clearly became taboo because anything one said that others that could be interpreted negatively reflected on one's highly honed sense of self-respect, propriety, and honor.

Histories say that during the long Choson dynasty (1392–1910), the demands of *chae-myun* were so powerful they contributed significantly to cultural, social, and economic stagnation because they prevented people from having free, open, and critical discussions about things of importance.

During this era, the only safe recourse was to say nothing and do nothing that might upset anyone or lead to changing the way things were done.

Face-saving is still extremely important to all South Koreans, especially to the older generations, but political and social freedom has unleashed the ambitions and dreams that South Koreans had to repress until the 1960s, and they could not change things fast enough.

Face-saving remains South Korea's "cultural lubricant," without which things cannot and will not run smoothly. Still today South Koreans continuously engage in *chae-myun* in all of their personal and business relationships, and foreigners in South Korea must do the same if they wish to succeed.

In simple terms, "face" refers to one's social and professional position, reputation, and self-image. It is of extreme importance to South Koreans that their "face" be protected and maintained. The use of respectful language, the extraordinary degree of politeness, the custom of heaping praise on people and of massaging their *kibun* (feelings) are parts of the overall process of avoiding any threat to one's self-image—as a man or a woman, as a competent worker, as a professional, or whatever. The downside of this cultural characteristic is that people avoid being critical when criticism is due, are excessive in their compliments, and put much more emphasis on form and appearance than on content or underlying reality.

The cultural need of South Koreans to protect their "face" is often misunderstood by foreigners, who are unfamiliar with this kind of etiquette. The foreign businessman in South Korea should keep in mind that while Koreans as a rule are genuinely friendly and often overly anxious to please, their efforts to maintain their own and others' face can cause serious problems if the foreigner presumes that what he sees and hears is what he is going to get.

Hospitality as Face

Koreans are famous for the hospitality they proffer to *sonnim* (sohn-neem), or guests, and where foreign guests are concerned, this hospitality can be so effusive and so aggressive, that it can be overwhelming.

One of the primary reasons for this level of hospitality is that it has long been equated with "face" or image. The more effusive the hospitality, the more face the host gained. And in earlier times, extending profuse hospitality was one of the only ways Koreans had of temporarily dispensing with the enforced frugality of their lifestyle and really enjoy themselves.

Hospitality in present-day South Korea extended to foreign guests and foreign business associates has a strong nationalistic element as well as cultural ramifications.

By extending an extraordinary level of hospitality to foreign guests, Koreans not only gain personal face, they also demonstrate unbounded pride in their country, its long culture, and its contemporary achievements.

In fact, some degree of South Korea's amazing economic achievements can be attributed to the almost compulsive hospitality they extend to their foreign business associates. Most foreigners who regularly visit or take up residence in South Korea become deeply attached to the Korean exuberance for life and the almost endless hospitality they receive.

Avoiding Shame

Christianized people around the world are threatened with the fires of Hell if they behave in a way not condoned by their religious leaders. They are taught and conditioned to follow the principles of Christianity based on a deep sense of guilt.

Institutionalized Korean behavior has never been based on divine standards or on a sense of guilt. Instead, it has been based on a sense of *changpi* (chahng-pee), or shame, as taught by Confucius.

Confucius was wise enough to understand that guilty feelings can be hidden, and that one can be guilty of the most heinous crimes and, if not caught and punished, walk around with his or her head held high, neither criticized nor ostracized by friends, family, or society at large.

In the Confucian concept, morality was based on one's daily behavior, something that was visible for all to see. Those who did not think and act in an acceptable Confucian way brought immediate shame to themselves, their families, and their communities.

In other words, Korean morality was traditionally based on following a prescribed physical etiquette, not on principles that could be interpreted differently and stretched or ignored without any consequence if you didn't get caught.

The power of a shame culture lies in a natural inclination for people to avoid causing emotional pain to themselves—pain that can be caused by being looked down upon by others, by being embarrassed, by being disgraced in the eyes of others—and in severe cases, being ostracized from one's family and community.

While there are some similarities in guilt and shame cultures, there are fundamental differences that guilt-ridden people have difficulty accepting. People in shame-centered cultures can get by with all kinds of "immoral" or antisocial behavior and not suffer the consequences as long as it doesn't become public or as long as it is something that is not considered shameful in their societies.

This means that people in shame cultures can lie, cheat, and do other things (that would give some Christians fits) without triggering any shame feelings as long as they follow the prescribed rules of physical etiquette in their relationships with others.

Said another way, feeling shame is primarily a social thing; feeling guilt is more of a spiritual thing. And because of that, shame is a more powerful deterrent to misbehavior than guilt.

Although a significant percentage of South Koreans profess to being Christians, and Christian concepts of right and wrong and the guilt syndrome are well-known by Koreans and have had a significant influence on Korean culture since the end of the 19th century, scratch any Korean and below a shallow layer of Christian guilt you will find a thick layer of Confucian shame.

One of the prime rules of doing business successfully in South Korea (not to mention dealings with government officials) is never, ever shame anyone.

The Unbearable Burden

We mentioned earlier that Korea traditionally had a *mangshin* (mahng-sheen), or shame culture, meaning that behavior was primarily controlled by an extraordinary sense of shame, which, in fact, was an unbearable burden that they went to extremes to avoid. This sense of shame, which is alive and well in present-day South Korea (although in a significantly reduced form), was a product of Confucianism, which taught that the highest morality was abiding by a strict form of etiquette that was based on hierarchical relationships between people.

The ongoing concern that South Koreans have with avoiding shame is one of the cultural factors that often complicates their relationships with Westerners, whose skins tend to be much thicker and often impervious to shame.

Among the things that Westerners do that South Koreans are likely to be shamed by is public criticism, being disrespectful toward them by manner or word, and underestimating their abilities (as perceived by South Koreans, of course).

Foreigners doing business in South Korea should keep in mind that shame, acutely felt, is far more effective in controlling behavior than the Western concept of guilt, which is easily contained or ignored altogether, at least in modern times.

The Shame of Failure

Because Koreans were programmed for centuries to shun independent thinking, individualistic behavior, and personal responsibility, they became extraordinarily sensitive to personal *shilpae* (sheel-pay), or failure, in any form.

There is a good side and a bad side to the Korean fear of personal failure. On the one hand, it drives them to be wary of personal responsibility and therefore be reluctant to think and act independently. But at the same time, it also drives them to work in groups with a diligence and compulsion that often goes well beyond the call of duty from the Western perspective.

Death before Dishonor

Westerners are familiar with the concept of choosing death over dishonor, but very few people in the West are ever put to the test, and those occasions when they do face this challenge are generally extreme, and more likely than not occur in times of war. In other words, the death-before-dishonor mindset is not a part of the cultural programming of Westerners.

In feudal Korea, on the other hand, ordinary Koreans were taught that upholding their *myongye* (m'yohng-eh), honor, or not being shamed, was of paramount importance and that without honor they were nothing.

In the Confucian-oriented society that prevailed in Korea until the 20th century, upholding one's honor meant scrupulously obeying all of the recognized customs and laws of society. In other words, the Confucian concept of honor was not a universally applicable moral code, but a matter of the social class, gender, age, and position of the individual. The guidelines for what was right and wrong in Korean society were absolute, so individual interpretations did not exist.

In this context, Koreans became culturally imbued with the belief that they had to uphold their honor at all times and at any cost. This meant they had to conform to the strict etiquette prescribed by custom and the feudal government: To dress well and appropriately for their class and station, to take all of their obligations seriously, to work diligently and hard, and to be concerned about the reputation of their family, their community, their clan, and their country—and to avoid shame at all cost.

Much of the energy and spirit that transformed South Korea from a feudal, agricultural society into a world-class industrial power in one generation derived from their intense feelings of personal and national honor.

To succeed in South Korea, foreign businesspeople, and diplomats in particular, must have a significant degree of knowledge about South Korean values, expectations, and behavior in the context of their ongoing need to maintain their *myongye*.

Peace of Mind

One of the most important ingredients in contemporary South Korean culture is subsumed in the world *anshim* (ahn-sheem), which literally means "peaceful heart," but may be translated as "peace of mind."

But the "peace of mind" inferred by *anshim* does not refer to the universal concept of harmony in thought and behavior in the Western sense. It refers to obeying the precise rules and customs of Korean behavior so there is no friction between people, no disputes, no fights, no hurt feelings.

Anshim remains the ideal of contemporary South Korean culture, and much of the social and business etiquette, as well as the ethics of South Korean behavior, are designed to create and sustain an environment of "peace of mind" in personal relations, business, and other public activities. The South Korean language itself is a primary vehicle for creating and sustaining *anshim*, in both the vocabulary that is used and the manner of its use.

A great deal of the behavior that outsiders consider irrational, ignorant, or disruptive in some way by South Koreans is a manifestation of the deep-seated need of Koreans to maintain the culturally-mandated *anshim*.

Some examples of this behavior include: an employee who keeps quiet about a mistake; an employee who does not complain about an obvious injustice; and businesspeople (as well as politicians) who misrepresent the facts to avoid upsetting *anshim*.

Anshim often demands that South Koreans express themselves indirectly, keep quiet when Westerners would speak up, and expect others to understand their true meanings and feelings from their common cultural background.

South Koreans, like most Westerners, are also culturally blind in that they generally expect foreigners to understand and accept their culturally-induced behavior, because that is the only way they can think and behave.

Much of the communication in South Korea is nonverbal and subliminal—and equates very well with what I call "cultural telepathy." There are certain things that people do and certain rules they obey that do not require conversation or explanation. They are simply understood and accepted without question.

Foreigners in South Korea can overcome some of the obstacles caused by the dictates of *anshim* by letting their Korean friends, contacts, or coworkers know that they are familiar with the requirements of *anshim* in Korean life, and will do their best to abide by them.

Situational Truth

The first Westerners arrived in Korea in the 1600s as a result of their ships floundering on the Korean coast in raging storms. When the survivors were finally allowed to leave the country, or managed to escape, they had one complaint in common: that Koreans were incapable of telling the truth.

What these early castaways had encountered was a culture in which *chongmal* (chohng-mahl), or truth, was situational or circumstantial, and was based on the existing realities of Korean life, rather than abstract principles. Truth was what people in power and the government said it was. The people of Korea at that time were simply not allowed to speak the truth in their personal relationships or any of their affairs—much less about things directly controlled by the government.

In my book, *Korea's Business & Cultural Code Words*, I describe this situation in the following terms: "The 'truth' in all matters was an artificially constructed political and social artifice that had been designed to preserve the harmony of a hierarchically arranged authoritarian society that denied personal individuality and human rights. All personal feelings and concerns were secondary to the interests of the state, which based its policies on a corrupted form of Confucianism that the government used to justify itself."

In this environment, a "truthful" response was whatever would sustain and enhance the harmonious behavior of the people within a culture where their attitudes and actions were controlled in detail—right down to how to hold chopsticks.

When these earlier Western visitors encountered this form of Korean reality they took it to mean that Koreans had no principles and no honor, and that they knowingly lied for malicious purposes rather than as a part of their normal behavior.

Present-day Koreans are perfectly aware of the differences between real truth and contrived truth, and when they are in "culture free" situations, such as when dealing with foreigners, their inclination is to tell the real truth. But in earlier times in purely Korean settings, they were under tremendous pressure to tailor the truth to maintain Korean-style harmony—to keep everything calm and smooth on the surface.

But this ancient way of maintaining harmony has been eroded by the dictates of a society that is less and less controlled by Confucian ethics, and more influenced by the hard facts and realities of democracy and capitalism.

Still, the foreign businessperson or diplomat in South Korea must have his or her "truth antenna" up at all times in order to avoid being misled, intentionally or otherwise, by the legacy of circumstantial truth that still lingers in the culture.

Justice South Korean Style

It often seems that the most popular word in the vocabulary of American businesspeople dealing with South Korea and other countries is "fair." That is especially interesting because until recent times there was no word in the Korean or Japanese languages for the word "fair."

In feudal Korean society, which did not officially end until late 1945 and was unofficially still present in the culture until the 1960s and beyond, the concepts of equality and fairness did not play any role in Korean culture.

Americans in particular have traditionally tried to enforce fairness with a justice system that has only been partially successful but is better than nothing. In Korea, the traditional justice system had an altogether different foundation and different purpose. It was designed to sustain the government and ruling powers, and to maintain a strict harmony and stability based on Confucian concepts.

In other words, *chongui* (chohng-we), or justice, was designed by and for the government, to keep the people under absolute control. Both responsibility and punishment were collective and often severe—something that seriously impedes innovation and progress.

Justice and fairness in the contemporary Western sense did not exist in Korea until well after the end of the Korean War in the early 1950s, when South Korean students began taking to the streets in massive and often violent demonstrations demanding that the laws be changed. It took many years, but it was high school and college students in South Korea who forced government leaders to break with traditions that went back thousands of years.

Justice and fairness in South Korea still have a nationalistic tint, and in some business cases they are aggressively weighted in favor of South Korea and Koreans, so it behooves foreigners doing business in South Korea to be very aware that the words justice and fairness do not necessarily mean the same thing in Korean terms.

Generally, justice in South Korea is based on what the judges and government agencies believe is best for South Korea as a country and for South Koreans as a people—from the viewpoint that in the past Koreans have suffered massive death and destruction at the hands of foreign powers and foreign ideologies.

Another important factor when considering notions of justice and fairness are the regional differences that impact on business, sometimes to the detriment of foreign companies. So it is important for foreigners to get local input from friendly staff or others who can help them adjust to local conditions.

The Communications Problem

Communication is, of course, a necessary foundation for understanding and cooperation, and while more and more South Koreans are being educated abroad and becoming bilingual, and the number who learn English in local schools is also increasing rapidly, the foreign businessman who does not learn some Korean is greatly limited in both his professional and social contacts.

Those who cannot communicate at all in Korean are severely handicapped in their ability to relate to and participate in life outside the narrow confines of the foreign community and world of international business.

Korean is generally described as difficult for English speakers to learn because it is unlike any Western language. Becoming fluent in Korean is a formidable task, but learning enough of the language to communicate on a basic level is easy enough that anyone of average ability can accomplish this limited goal in two or three months of daily sustained study.

Korean is mostly made up of "pure Korean" and Chinese words, along with a sizable number of terms borrowed from Japanese and English. The Korean language is called *Hangugo* (hahn-guu-go) in Korean. The alphabet, *Hangul*, was created by a team of scholars in the 1400s at the behest of King Sejong. There are 14 consonants and 10 vowels in the language. Various combinations of these make up approximately 54 sounds or syllables. (See the back of this book for a list of these syllables and a pronunciation chart.)

Over the centuries, very few Westerners learned the Korean language, resulting in Koreans believing that it was simply too difficult for foreigners to grasp. As recently as the 1970s, Korean-speaking Westerners were so rare that most Koreans were amazed to encounter one who was able to speak the language—and they would often fail to understand the Korean-speaking foreigner because they simply couldn't conceive of that being possible.

Anecdotes of Westerners speaking quite fluent Korean but getting only a blank stare in return were commonplace. This situation has changed considerably since the 1970s. A significant percentage of the foreign businessmen stationed in South Korea are students of the language and some of them speak it very well. South Koreans in rural areas may still be surprised to hear Korean spoken by a foreigner, but this is no longer the case in the cities.

Because of the development of a superior-inferior social structure and a highly refined system of etiquette between and among classes of people, several different levels of language were also developed to distinguish between individuals and classes. The three most important basic levels of the language are an extraordinarily polite form used when addressing superiors, an intimate or familiar form for addressing close friends or equals, and a rough form used when speaking to people on a lower social level.

Becoming fully fluent in Korean therefore means that one has to master these various levels, which is almost like learning three related but different languages. Fortunately, foreigners who are less than fluent are generally excused from this very strict social requirement and can get by with the use of familiar Korean in most situations. There are occasions, however, when the use of familiar speech is not appropriate and it is better either to speak in English or to remain silent.

As is often the case in the languages of Asia, there are a number of peculiarities in Korean and its use that must be quickly mastered by the foreigner who attempts to use the language on any level. It is not common to use the single word "no" as a response, since "no" on its own is regarded as too abrupt and too impolite. In Korean the appropriate response to a negative question is a negative—i.e., If you say, "Don't you know his phone number?" The answer may be "Yes" (meaning yes, you are right. I don't know his phone number).

This can cause both confusion and frustration, and can be avoided by phrasing all questions in the positive form. "No" is one of the most commonly used words in the English language, but it is virtually untranslatable in Korean and gives a very negative impression when used—because Koreans tend to associate its use with being uncertain and unable to make up one's mind.

Until the 1980s and 1990s, American expatriate businesspeople were notorious for not knowing, and not making any attempt to learn, local languages. That ignoble part of the American mindset has finally yielded to logic. Virtually all American businesspeople stationed in South Korea are now avid students of the Korean language.

The Korean standard for communicating with others is expressed in the phrase, *uishin jonshin* (we-sheen joan-sheen), which literally means "from my heart to your heart" or "heart to heart." In its Korean context it is the type and level of communication that takes place nonverbally, and is a kind of cultural telepathy.

Because they are products of an intensely personal culture that homogenizes them, Koreans often know what the other person is thinking without the use of words. It is the type of communicating they are naturally familiar with, and they often run into difficulty in dealing with foreigners because they take it for granted that the foreigner is on the same wavelength and is "receiving" their messages.

The Great Ethical Divide

The one ethical area that probably causes Western businesspeople more frustration than anything else in the Korean social system is the dichotomy between fairness and loyalty. To Westerners, particularly Americans, the bedrock of their ethical philosophy is fairness. This word is probably used more often than any other in our business discussions and negotiations.

In South Korea, however, personal loyalty often takes precedence over fairness. When this difference in ethical codes is applied to business relationships, the results are very different, to say the least. It is therefore vital that foreigners keep this distinctive Korean cultural value in mind at all times and anticipate the effect it will have on everything they do in South Korea, from dealing with government officials to haggling with a landlord over the cost of an apartment.

This is another area in which Westerners with limited cross-cultural experience typically make one error after another by either ignoring the fairness-loyalty factor altogether or playing it down because their inclination is to believe that everyone automatically understands and appreciates the concept of fairness, and will just as automatically accept it as the foundation for any business relationship.

The Kindness Trap

South Koreans are legendary for their kindness and hospitality. It is one of their strongest cultural traditions—and is now used unabashedly in their diplomacy and business with the rest of the world. Foreign visitors are entertained and pampered, often to the point that they are no longer able to make objective decisions. This gives South Koreans a tremendous advantage, especially where Americans are concerned, since we feel such an overwhelming obligation to reciprocate by being less critical and more cooperative in helping them achieve what they want.

Since it is both financially and emotionally difficult for the foreign visitor to match the generosity of South Korean hosts, it frequently becomes necessary to limit the amount of hospitality one accepts, and to take extra steps to get even with some kind of special gift.

Class Consciousness and School Ties

Americans and other Westerners are racially and color conscious, but Americans are generally not class conscious—something that can have a negative impact on their hiring and managing employees in South Korea.

Unless cautioned and informed by someone with South Korean experience, American managers are likely to encounter problems as a result of the ongoing existence and role of social class in any group of Korean employees. In the past, American managers who had some knowledge of Korean culture have attempted to pre-empt future problems by lecturing new Korean employees on democracy, and informing them that class would play no role in the management of the company.

While Korean employees surely understood and appreciated

the principles of such lectures the lectures invariably had little if any affect on their attitudes and behavior, both deeply embedded in their psyche and not subject to being switched off at will.

While the cultural character of younger, educated South Koreans has changed and continues to change, in virtually any group there will be class differences that continue to influence the behavior of every individual in the group.

Newcomers setting up operations in South Korea should get local input in both hiring and managing Korean staff—again, preferably from a professional employment agency instead of through personal contacts.

Another key factor in managing in South Korea, already mentioned several times, is the role of *tongchang hoe* (tohng-chahng hoh-eh), or alumni groups. School ties, especially among individuals who attended the same schools from primary grades through university, are especially strong, often approaching the importance of blood-ties.

Within large companies that hire from the same schools these groups form generational layers based on longevity—a factor that perpetuates the junior-senior relationship throughout their working lives, and generally contributes to loyalty and diligence in attitudes and performance. These same generational layers of alumni groups also play a vital role between companies, since they facilitate communication and cooperation between the companies.

Foreign companies going into South Korea should be aware of this factor, and take advantage by hiring fresh graduates from schools with former graduates who are well-placed in business and the government. Corporate managers and executives who have junior alumni brothers in high government offices have a special advantage, since the etiquette and ethics that control junior-senior relationships in South Korea remain a powerful force in society.

Juniors and Seniors

Despite the Western façade presented by contemporary South Korean society and the business infrastructure, once you get beneath the façade many of Korea's traditional cultural customs and habits are still very much in evidence.

One of the most important of the cultural factors in feudal South Korea's hierarchically structured society was the *sonbae* (sohn-bay) and *hubae* (huuh-bay), or senior-junior system of ranking people. In this system, there were no equals. Everyone, except the king, was higher or lower than somebody else, and this gradation determined the individual's life to an incredible degree.

All of the traditional factors that determined one's status in terms of *sonbae* and *hubae* are still in use in contemporary South Korean society, although in weakened form in certain areas. These factors include sex, age, family background, and schools attended.

Again, South Korean companies and other organizations function very much like military squads, companies, regiments, and divisions, with corresponding ranks based primarily on the above factors, plus longevity. Upper level managers and executives invariably are made up of individuals who come from elite family backgrounds and the ranking high schools and universities.

Differences in rank within organizations of all kinds are taken seriously, and the behavior of people on all levels is regimented just as it is in military life. The social credentials as well as attitude and behavior play a role in promotions to upper levels of management.

Foreign companies hiring staff in South Korea should be well informed about the social and educational background of employee candidates because their background will influence the way others view and treat the company. Foreign managers should also be wary of hiring and mixing staff whose backgrounds are dissimilar in order to avoid possible friction.

One source of potential problems is to put someone of a lower social rank over an employee whose social pedigree—class and education—is higher. This may be done, however, if the higher ranked employee is significantly older and obviously more experienced than the other individual.

South Korean companies make every effort to take advantage of the obligatory ties that exist among senior and junior graduates of the same high schools and universities, since these ties mean they are much more likely to be loyal and work together smoothly.

Foreign companies setting up in South Korea are advised to get professional assistance in formulating their work rules and in hiring personnel, to avoid cultural friction. They should also be wary of depending on a single South Korean contact they may have to source potential employees, since he or she is likely to pick family members, relatives, and friends.

The Power of Social Debts

Another of South Korea's cultural legacies from its Confucian past is expressed in the term *unhye* (uhn-heh), which means "benefits," and is extrapolated to cover the "social debts" that people incur and are under a heavy moral obligation to repay.

Unhye covers the debt that people owe to their parents, their teachers, their schoolmates, their employers—to anyone, in fact, from whom they have received some kind of benefit that contributes to their livelihood and life goals.

Parents and teachers in particular have a strong moral right to expect that those whom they have benefited will repay them throughout their lives. University professors traditionally use their influence with former students in high positions in government and industry to hire or find jobs for newly graduated students, thus continuing the circle of *unhye*.

Foreign businesspeople and others can build up the same kind of "social capital" by doing favors for individual Koreans and Korean families. Acting as the host for a Korean student studying abroad ensures that the family will do everything possible to repay the benefit.

The Stubborn Syndrome

A national attribute of South Koreans that all foreigners encounter at one time or another—and often on a daily basis—is a natural propensity for *ogi* (oh-ghee) or stubbornness.

It seems obvious that the stubbornness that characterizes Koreans is a legacy of all the hardships they had to endure over the millennia, from the weather and other natural disasters to occupation by foreign invaders and the pain and suffering imposed on them by their own governments.

The literal meaning of *ogi* is "unyielding spirit," and that describes Koreans to a T. Among the manifestations of this stubbornness is a general unwillingness to admit making a mistake, or to admit that they are not capable of doing something.

These two attributes are, of course, exactly the opposite of the etiquette and ethics of Americans and Western Europeans. Our way is to admit mistakes, do everything possible to minimize any damage, and get on with it.

Koreans typically take great pride in their stubbornness, seeing it as the quality that has allowed them to survive and to succeed where so many others have failed. Still, Korean businesspeople are very much aware that this cultural factor is often upsetting to foreigners, and they continuously counsel patience. They also typically add that to succeed in South Korea you need an iron butt (because of so many long meetings) and an iron stomach (to endure all the alcohol that is typically consumed in the process of establishing and maintaining business relationships).

There is no simple or short way of getting by the *ogi* of Koreans. It is a deeply embedded state of mind that yields only gradually to patience and persistence—if ever. The decades long *ogi* of the North Korean government is as good or as bad an example as you can find, depending on which side of the demarcation line you are on.

Doing Things by the Book

Westerners, Americans in particular, are familiar with the saying, "doing things by the book"—which seems to be most commonly used in the military and in law enforcement, where independent thinking and initiative are frowned on.

Well, Westerners who do things by the book are babes-in-the-woods when compared to the South Koreans. In Korea, for some 2,000 years or more years, there has been an exact, precise *chongshik* (chohng-sheek) process, or procedure, for doing things, applied to virtually every action in life.

To paraphrase my description of this culturally laden term in *Korea's Business & Cultural Code Words*:

"For century after century Koreans were physically, emotionally, and intellectually programmed in all of the *chongshik* making up the Korean lifestyle—from worshiping, bowing, sitting, eating, performing household chores, and working, to the way they used the Korean language."

This conditioning in attitudes and behavior was so pervasive that it gradually became the foundation of the Korean lifestyle, so integrated into Korean culture that the two could not be separated. It was something that was automatically taught to each child, directly and indirectly, from infancy, and thus became an integral part of his or her character and personality.

Most South Koreans today still do things "by the book" to a much greater degree than Americans and other Westerners. It is still very much a part of formal ceremonies, business and diplomatic protocol, cultural rites, festivals, etc.

This ongoing cultural factor may not be inherently bad, but it often formalizes meetings and other endeavors to the point that it becomes a serious drag on efficiency, spontaneity, and innovation. Even the most mundane things often must be "done by the book," almost always resulting in complications and delays.

Again because of the dictates of democracy, capitalism, and an economy that is rapidly becoming global, major corporations and the South Korean government are making a serious effort to reduce the formality and complexities of many procedures.

But Koreans as a whole are not likely to disavow all of their traditional *chongshik* because they are too integrated into the lifestyle and culture and still defines the character and behavior of most South Koreans.

Dealing with Facts

Western businesspeople claim to love facts; South Koreans typically put human feelings first. The gap separating the two sides can therefore be enormous. Even when the gap is narrow, it can blunt the building of a new relationship, and gradually undermine one that has been going on for years.

Another gap that often separates Westerners and Koreans is the aforementioned Western concept of fairness. What is fair to a Westerner may not be fair to a Korean. Fairness in the Korean mindset tends to be based on personal factors; not on the hard, dry facts, mutual equality, and mutual benefits that motivate Westerners.

In Korea, fairness was traditionally based on class, sex, age, and position, with all of the inferior-superior elements that made up their hierarchical society. Much of this mindset has gone by the wayside, but there are still fundamental differences in the way Koreans and Westerners measure fairness.

Foreign businesspeople in South Korea can generally work around this difference by first emphasizing the personal, human elements of their relationship, and the personal facets of projects or programs, and then bringing in the facts of the situation.

Handled with diplomacy and a true appreciation of the feelings of Koreans, it is almost always possible to get down to the hard facts of a relationship that includes the full understanding and cooperation of the Korean side. It is more in the presentation than absolute differences in methods and goals.

When "Maybe" Means "No"

For centuries Koreans were meticulously programmed to avoid confrontations, ultimatums, and clear-cut commitments as a means of ensuring harmony in society. To achieve this goal, the people were conditioned to speak in vague terms that could be interpreted in a number of ways, or not to speak at all.

In the country's hierarchically structured society where absolute rules defined inferior-superior relationships, speaking in clear, unambiguous terms, telling the truth, or making a critical comment could have seriously negative repercussions, and in worst-case scenarios be life-threatening.

In this environment, Koreans learned to avoid saying no, and to divine the meaning and intent of others through cultural intuition, or "cultural telepathy."

Saying *anio* (ahn-n'yoh), or no, outright was regarded as impolite, if not insulting.

When the first Westerners to visit Korea encountered this kind of behavior they immediately assumed that Koreans were dishonest, devious, and could not be trusted.

The social imperative for ambiguous speech has eroded significantly in contemporary South Korea, especially among those who are involved in international business, but it continues to be an important cultural factor in business and politics, and must be taken into account.

One of the obvious ways to bring negotiations to a close and get clear-cut commitments is to ask that they be put in official documents that are signed by the responsible people. If the documents are not forthcoming, the real situation is not clear.

Personal Responsibility

It was not until the 1960s and 1970s that South Koreans began to win and receive the right to behave as individuals for the first time in the history of the country.

Prior to these fundamental changes in South Korean society, the people were simply not allowed to think or act like individuals. They were bonded to their families, to their communities, to the authorities, and to traditional customs, and had to act in unison with them.

In this system individual South Koreans could not develop a sense of personal *chaegim* (chay-geem), or responsibility. Responsibility was collective—based first on the family, then on the community, then the clan.

The father and the family as a whole were responsible for the attitudes and conduct of every member of the family—not only in enforcing the laws and customs of the day, but also accepting collective punishment when any member behaved in a disruptive manner.

Present-day South Koreans are still conditioned to believe in collective responsibility, a factor that impacts directly and fundamentally on their social and business behavior—and often puts them at odds with Western thinking and expectations.

In broad terms, Westerners expect individuals to take personal responsibility for their attitudes and actions. South Koreans continue to take a more collective approach to all *chaegim*, especially in work related situations.

South Korean executives and mangers generally give an impression of authoritative figures who can and do give orders on their own because they are invariably surrounded by cadres of secretaries and aides who respond to their orders like marine recruits. But in reality, it is generally only strong-minded company founders who can give orders like a military commander.

While there is a gradual shift in some companies to decision-making by individuals, most executives and managers can act only after they achieve a consensus within their departments.

More and more South Koreans are also assuming personal responsibility for their actions in family as well as business affairs, but it will surely be a number of generations before the influence of collective *chaegim* has diminished to the extent that it has in the West.

Dealing with "Big Brother"

In South Korea, the national interest often takes precedence over private business, and the government plays a key role in most industries by significantly influencing, or outright controlling, who can do what and how it is done. The government exercises its influence and control through a variety of laws, long precedent, and the willing cooperation and support of much of the South Korean business community.

The objective of the South Korean government is to do everything possible to encourage the continuing growth of the economy and development of the national infrastructure so the entire nation benefits, rather than allow a free-for-all atmosphere which results in extraordinary growth in some areas but disruptions or deteriorations in others.

Within the context of this overall government policy, individual businesspeople and enterprises are allowed the freedom to grow as fast as they can and make as much profit as possible. To keep industrial and social development going forward in the direction it desires, the government makes ready use of all of its powers. Some of the methods used by the government (and by South Korean companies in their dealings with foreign partners) to get its way include: enforcing import or export restrictions; denying or delaying licensing applications; causing customs clearance difficulties; refusing to renew visas; stopping payments; breaking contracts, and so on.

Despite the real and apparent handicaps this policy represents to foreign companies wanting to do business in South Korea, the overall climate for foreign investment and business activity in the country is favorable, and offers special opportunities to those who are able and willing to approach the market with an open mind, goodwill, a great deal of flexibility, determination, and patience.

At the same time, there are many South Korean businessmen, government officials, and others who are strongly opposed to welcoming any more foreign businessmen in the country because of potential danger to its security and continuing economic success—in direct contradiction to the public policies of the government. These sentiments are often responsible for the "invisible barriers" that foreign businessmen frequently encounter in South Korea.

Because these conflicting positions and practices further complicate the relationship between businessmen and the government, it is vital that the foreign businessman who hopes to succeed in South Korea understands the psychology of South Korean behavior and masters some of the techniques for dealing with individuals on many levels in a variety of different ministries or agencies.

The first and probably most important lesson the foreign businessman must learn is that individual government officials cannot be approached on a strictly rational, practical, or policy-focused basis. Everything is handled on a case-by-case and very personal basis. Furthermore, officials on different levels in the same agencies and ministries will interpret the same laws and factors differently, often resulting in substantial delays before an application or proposal can be steered through the government red tape.

Probably the second most important lesson is that neither the ethical nor the legal system in South Korea provides the kind or depth of security and protection that the typical Western businessman expects. This includes the view and treatment of contracts, patents, copyrights, and other legal matters.

The third most important lesson may well be that even after everything has been approved and seems to be in order, the whole thing can come apart and have to be renegotiated because, in the view of some government official or company executive, circumstances have changed and the original agreement is no longer valid. This means, of course, that the successful businessperson in South Korea must remain in regular communication with everyone even remotely connected or involved in his business in order to remain current on their thinking and plans and to be able to anticipate their actions.

Again this comes down to establishing and nurturing personal relations with company managers and government officials on all the appropriate levels in all the concerned ministries or agencies. This entails a great deal of one's personal time as well as expenditures for drinks, meals, and other expenses. The developing and nurturing of personal relations of this type cannot be done casually or taken for granted. It is a serious business.

Another aspect of the personal side of business in South Korea is that the foreign businessman, no matter what his experience or credentials in his home country, must "re-prove" himself in South Korea in terms that are acceptable to South Koreans. He must earn the respect and loyalty of Korean associates and employees through his professional skills and knowledge, through his approach to developing and maintaining personal relations, by not breaking any of the taboos of Korean society, by demonstrating sincerity, and appreciation for Korean sensitivities.

It is especially important for the foreign employer in South Korea to treat his Korean staff with enlightened, personal concern that keeps them loyal and motivated. This includes following expected procedures in management and otherwise dealing with employees.

The Guiding Hand of Government
In the words of a foreign businessman with long experience in South Korea, "the government is everywhere," meaning there is virtually no area of business that is free of governmental influence or outright guidance.

The Korean term for the influence the government exercises over business is *haengjung chido* (hang-jung chee-doh), which means "administrative guidance." This influence is exercised through the control of licenses, import and export quotas, taxes, government financing, and so on. In addition, there are numerous *naekyu* (nay-k'yuu) or "unwritten laws," that agencies and ministries use to influence and/or control the economy.

One of the "unwritten laws" that many businesses encounter, both Korean and foreign, goes by the picturesque name of *gara muingeida* (gah-rah muun-gay-dah), which translates as "crushing with one's rear end." In other words, killing applications or proposals by "sitting on them" until the petitioner gives up.

Another descriptive term for government inaction is *jajungga bakwi dolligi* (jah-juung-gah bahk-wee dohol-lee-ghee), or "pedaling on a stationary bike."

The *naekyu* may or may not be applied, and may also be applied in a different manner or to different degrees by different individuals. This is one of the reasons that it is so important for foreign businessmen to have the input and guidance of someone who has been on the scene for a long time and knows how to get around and through the maze of *naekyu*.

Another factor effecting the lives and fortunes of businesses in South Korea is the presence of hundreds of *hyopoe* (h'yahp-poh-eh), or associations, many of them sponsored by the government and therefore quasi-government agencies.

There is an association for virtually every industry and profession in South Korea, all of which are required to operate within guidelines established by the government. But not all of them are burdensome to business.

Some maintain extensive data banks of information on specific industries, and provide free staff help to businesspeople seeking such information, along with assisting them in setting up appointments.

The government and the state-sponsored associations also follow the age-old practice of bringing political, economic, and social leverage against companies to prevail upon them to make *kibu* (kee-buu), or donations, to various causes.

According to the local press, many of these donations end up in the pockets of politicians and political parties.

While the machinations of the South Korean government and

its agents are often criticized by local and foreign businesspeople, overall the results of this "Big Brother" approach to the economy has been a major factor in South Korea's rise to economic prominence.

The Role of Friends in Business

One of the primary keys to doing business successfully in South Korea—and enjoying the process—is having lots of *chingu* (cheen-guu), which means "friends."

Having a wide circle of friends and friendships is something new to South Korea. During the long Choson dynasty and, for that matter, during the Japanese occupation of South Korea from 1910 to 1945, friends and friendships outside of one's family and kin were rare.

During the Choson period, men and women lived virtually separate lives. Relationships for women were especially limited to members of their own families and close kin. In urban areas, women were confined to their homes during the day, and could visit female relatives only for a few hours at night, when men were required to stay indoors. Social customs also restricted the relationships of men to a narrow circle.

This factor was one of a number of things that limited economic, political, and social progress in Korea until modern times. It was not until the feudal class system was abolished and the introduction of Western-type companies into Korea at the end of the 19th century that the limitations on friendships outside of family and kin circles began to break down; and this new freedom applied mostly to males.

Despite all of the changes that have occurred in Korea, especially since the end of World War II and the occupation of Korea by Japan, establishing new friendships in South Korea is not the casual thing that it is in the West. Except among the young, it is still regarded as a matter that requires serious thought because of obligations that might result.

But because Koreans do not feel comfortable or safe in doing business with strangers, they have literally been forced to go out and establish friendly relationships with large numbers of people in industry and in the government—something they do deliberately, with caution, and after careful planning.

South Koreans do not have any qualms about quickly establishing relationships with foreigners because there is little or no cultural baggage attached to such friendships. They are, however, discriminating in who they become friends with. Foreigners whose character, personality, and attitudes do not measure up to their standards don't make the cut.

The Importance of Sincerity

Cultural gaps between South Koreans and foreigners, especially Westerners, are often wide enough that inexperienced and insensitive people fall into them. One of the problems that both sides have to work to overcome is the perception that the other side is not to be trusted.

In judging others, again especially Westerners, Koreans generally put *chinshim* (cheen-sheem), or sincerity, high on the list of required attributes. Those who do not measure up to the standards expected by Koreans will not have an easy time of it. The catch comes with what Koreans mean by *chinshim*—which, as it turns out not surprisingly, is often quite different from what Westerners mean by sincerity.

Westerners think of sincerity as being open, honest, and straightforward. To Koreans, being *chinshim* (which literally means "true heart") is being true to all of their cultural expectations; that is, a person who is *chinshim* will be unselfish, unscrupulously honest, loyal to superiors, hardworking, and willing to make whatever sacrifices are necessary to succeed in any work or enterprise.

Expressed another way, being sincere in the Korean context means not doing anything that would harm or shame others; not doing anything that would damage an enterprise or a relationship; and not rocking the boat—a concept that is quite different, and much more comprehensive, than the Western perspective.

This means that the foreign businessperson who wants to be accepted as *chinshim* must be able and willing to do things the Korean way. Or be well enough versed in the ins and outs of

Korean culture to explain his or her perspective in terms that are acceptable to Koreans—that will benefit rather than damage the enterprise.

South Koreans automatically measure the *chinshim* of everyone they meet, and their "sincerity" radar is tuned up to the maximum when they meet foreigners for the first time.

Foreigners who want to improve their chances of making a good impression on new Korean contacts can do so by commenting that they are well aware of the importance of *chinshim* in establishing and maintaining positive relationships, and are committed to practicing it.

The Self-Reliant Syndrome

One of the most interesting, and significant, terms in the vocabulary of Korean businesspeople and politicians is *juche* (juu-cheh), which may be translated as self-reliant or self-sufficient.

The concept of *juche* is especially interesting because until well into the 20th century Koreans were not permitted to be self-sufficient across the board. The majority had to produce their own food and clothing, but beyond that, what they could do was strictly limited by law and by tradition. Further, the *juche* that existed in feudal Korea was collective rather than individual—based first on the entire family, and then on the community.

But because of the restrictions on individual self-reliance throughout Korean history, this was one of the motivations and desires that erupted with extraordinary energy when the people were finally freed from governmental and Confucian bonds.

Since the 1960s, South Koreans as a whole have strived with amazing industry to become self-reliant through education and work. On the business side, corporations expanded into virtually every facet of production and marketing in order to be self-sufficient—a move that worked like a miracle for several decades, but became a serious handicap when the huge conglomerates began to face stiff competition from abroad.

Probably the most extreme example of *juche* occurred in North Korea, where the Communist leader Kim Il-sung followed a three-pronged approach to *juche* in the foundation of the economy. His whole political philosophy was based on independence, self-sufficiency, and self-defense, an approach that doomed the people of North Korea to a level of poverty and suffering rare in the world today.

Juche as practiced in South Korea today—an obsession with getting an education and working with extraordinary energy to achieve a higher standard of living—remains a positive force that continues to energize the people and the government, and contributes to the goals of foreign companies doing business in South Korea.

CHAPTER FOUR

Korean Business Culture Today

The business environment in South Korea, a very small country with a large population, is intensely competitive, not only among the best workers and professionals, but also in terms of the allocation of space, licenses, and other factors making up a sophisticated business structure. Since this competitive factor is combined with a very personal approach to business, the whole business environment is susceptible to what international consultant Jang Song-hyon calls "irregular practices."

Jang says the extraordinary degree of competition and the personal nature of business in South Korea has resulted in a mentality in which the end justifies the means, and that the moral implications of much of the business behavior in South Korea today are blurred.

It is especially difficult for the newly arrived Western businessman to function effectively in South Korea because of the emotional, sensitive, and shifting nature of the business environment. The best possible approach is for the newcomer to enlist the aid of an experienced local consultant and go-between who is a respected and influential part of the business community and can manipulate his way through the maze of personal relationships involved in day-to-day business affairs.

This local representative may be an agent, a joint-venture partner, a broker, or a consultant, but he must be someone in whom the inexperienced foreign businessman can put complete faith to say and do the rights things on his behalf. Otherwise, the results can be disastrous.

Another factor continuously emphasized by such knowledgeable consultants as Jang is the importance of public image to the foreign company. "Foreign businessmen should give prominent consideration to the public image of their company. Many hurdles can be surmounted if the public relations of a corporation are effective in developing a strong, favorable image," Jang said.

As is so often the case in foreign ventures by American companies, the larger the company the more difficult it seems for it to make adaptations to fit into the South Korean political and business environment. One veteran observer said that American bankers in South Korea were the most rigid and inflexible of all. "You can recognize them on the street," he said. "Their inflexibility causes them so many problems it is unbelievable, and yet they persist."

Manners as Morality

Traditionally, in South Korea the officially prescribed *taedo* (tay-doh), or manners, were equated with morality. Those who conducted themselves in the manner mandated by the Confucian-oriented government were regarded as upright, fine people, while those who failed to follow the prescribed etiquette were regarded as immoral and subject to a variety of official and social sanctions.

In this context, the morality of individual South Koreans was visible for all to see. Failure to behave in the prescribed manner was so glaring that even the smallest deviation from the correct form and tone was immediately obvious to all.

This kind of morality system—as opposed to the Western kind, which is mostly based on an internal, invisible standard—made South Koreans among the best behaved of all people. While present-day South Koreans are far less manner-bound than previous generations, an impressive level of traditional etiquette is still alive and well, and distinguishes Koreans from Americans and other Westerners, who are much more informal in their behavior.

South Korean etiquette also has a powerful influence on foreigners who take up residence in the country. It affects their thinking as well as their behavior. Some make a conscious effort to adopt South Korean manners; in others the process is unconscious.

Foreigners should keep in mind that being able to act like a South Korean, including speaking the language well, is not always an advantage. South Koreans tend to treat Korean-acting foreigners like they treat other Koreans—which can range from being rude to ignoring them when there is no established relationship.

It is far more advantageous to remain in the "guest category," even if you know the etiquette and language, and benefit from the deeply entrenched custom of Koreans to treat all foreigners like guests no matter how long they may have been in the country.

Circumstantial Ethics

In traditional Korean culture, *todok* (toh-dohk), or ethics, was seen as an aspect of etiquette, not a clearly defined set of principles that distinguished between right and wrong in the Western sense.

There were, of course, ethics in feudal Korea, but rather than being universal principles of conduct, they consisted of the Confucian-based rules of behavior prescribed by the government for a hierarchically structured society that was designed to be harmonious by denying people the right to think and act independently.

In other words, Korean *todok* was a personalized set of circumstantial rules that applied to individuals in relation to their families, kin, friends, neighbors, and the government—rules designed to prevent any kind of behavior that would result in disharmony and threaten the government.

In this context, all emotional expression was minutely controlled. Love, in particularly, was taboo because it invariably leads to emotional behavior that cannot be predicted.

Because *todok* forbids individual thinking and acting, it resulted in Korean society remaining frozen in a virtual time-warp for several hundred years. Almost nothing changed from the early decades of the Choson dynasty, founded in 1392, until the 1890s.

With the introduction of democracy and Western style capitalism into South Korea in the middle of the 20th century, the imagination and inherent talents of Koreans were unleashed for the first time in the history of the country—with results that are obvious to the world.

But the age-old Korean system of circumstance-centered morality has not disappeared. In fact, as long as there is significant tolerance for a certain level of arbitrary, unfair, and unjust behavior, it can be a major advantage for an individual, a company, and a country to adjust morality to fit the situation—as was dramatically demonstrated in the recent history of Japan and China.

Foreign businesspeople dealing with South Korea generally have no problem recognizing when they are presented with a *todok* situation. The best recourse is to diplomatically, clearly, and succinctly point out the differences in the Korean scenario and reality, step back, and wait patiently for the other side to adjust their position.

Repeating yourself (as Americans tend to do when they come to an obstacle) hardly ever helps and often harms, especially since there is a tendency to compromise a bit with each repetition.

The Perils of *Pipyong*

Pipyong (peep-yohng) is the Korean word for criticism, and refers to one of the most sensitive areas of the Korean character. Until the feudal system really began to come apart in the 1960s, superiors could humiliate and criticize inferiors, but it was strictly taboo for an inferior to criticize a superior.

This system naturally helped to perpetuate the inferior-superior hierarchical form of Korean society, the corruption that existed on every level of government, and the ineptitude of many officials. It also helped to sustain one of the greatest emotional, spiritual, and intellectual burdens ordinary Koreans were forced to live with for centuries.

The higher ranking an individual, the more immune he was to criticism, and there were severe sanctions against anyone breaking this taboo. Interestingly, until recent times, artists and writers were included among those who were not to be criticized—because it was felt that any criticism would result in them giving up in their efforts to achieve perfection in their work.

Pipyong is no longer officially taboo in South Korea, and in the political arena the volume and vehemence of criticism heaped on government offices, from the top down, is unbounded. In commercial enterprises, however, it is still uncommon for inferiors to criticize their superiors.

But in some companies, a typical management technique is for managers and executives to publicly criticize employees, individually and in groups, who have made mistakes in the strongest possible terms—the rationale being that such severe public reprimands will result in them redoubling their efforts to avoid mistakes in the future and be more productive.

This is pure Confucian psychology, and it obviously works in South Korean settings, but foreign managers in South Korea are strongly advised against using the technique. Employees will take it from Korean bosses but not foreign bosses.

Foreign managers should exercise great care in ensuring that any criticisms are offered in strict privacy. In pep talks to groups, foreign managers may, however, safely express dissatisfaction with overall performance in diplomatic, general terms, including themselves in the blame and the need for improvement.

The Ethics of Revenge

One of the legacies of feudal Korea that has survived, in watered down form, is the cultural—and human—compulsion to take revenge when one is wronged. The traditional etiquette and ethics of pre-modern Korea was such that the people became exceedingly sensitive to any behavior that shamed them or put them in a bad light—a situation that could only be wiped clean by *poksu* (pohk-suu), or revenge, of some kind.

Extreme competition between families, communities, clans, and government agencies, endemic during Korea's long feudal age, was the original cause for much of the revenge mentality that persists in Korean society.

Most present-day South Koreans are no longer as thin-skinned as their ancestors, but *poksu* and *moryak* (moh-r'yahk), or "revenge plot," are still something that people have to be aware of and concerned about, especially foreigners who may unintentionally shame or insult someone.

Some situations in foreign-owned and managed companies can result in acts of revenge against the foreigners concerned. Typical examples might include: if their attitude and behavior is perceived as arrogant; if they appear to be incompetent and yet insist on doing things their way; blaming their employees for failures; and not being sensitive and responsive to the class and competency differences in their staff.

In worst-case scenarios, aggressive individuals have been known to undermine the efforts of their foreign bosses in a concerted effort to get them removed and take their places. These ploys are likely to work because in a South Korean cultural context, strong, aggressive individuals invariably attract supporters.

Here again, the only recourse for foreign managers in South Korea is to attempt to be totally frank and open with employees, make sure that the lines of communication are always open, never show favoritism to anyone (such as those who speak English or very attractive females).

In larger operations this is another circumstance when having a senior South Korean mentor or consultant on hand can prevent serious consequences.

The Jealousy Virus

In the Confucian concept of an ideal society jealousy of any kind is immoral. Thus, in pre-democratic Korea, wives were programmed not to be jealous of their husbands, and people as a whole were enjoined against being jealous of anyone for any reason.

Because there were built-in basic differences in the lifestyles of the common people and the ruling elite, and outwardly demonstrating or voicing any envy or jealousy was an absolute taboo, most of the people seethed with repressed jealousy. Any sign of superiority in intelligence or skill, or of a family getting ahead of others in a community, was viewed with hateful spite.

This extreme form of prejudice is still visible in South Korean society, and is one of the things that now motivates South Koreans to better themselves so that no one can look down on them. Also on the negative side, when individuals cannot keep up with or pass others there is a tendency for them to try to bring the others back down to their level.

Foreigners living in South Korea must be sensitive to the jealousy syndrome that still impacts on Korean attitudes and behavior, and take special care not to put on superior airs. This especially applies to interacting with government officials, and in the treatment of employees. Behaving in a conspicuously favorable manner toward a particular employee, for example, will invariably stir up jealousy among the rest of the staff.

Present-day South Korean women are especially jealous when it comes to the behavior of boyfriends and husbands—a visceral reaction to the anti-jealousy taboo that still exists in the culture. And this reaction can be especially severe when the males involved are Westerners.

Honoring Superiors

In feudal Korea people were primarily valued for their willing acceptance of all of the customs and traditions that made up the Korean way—not for their personal skills or accomplishments.

This ancient Confucian precept virtually guaranteed that any self-esteem felt by common people came from an absolute adherence to the cultural and political rules that applied to their social class, sex, age, order of birth, education, and occupation. With only a few exceptions, personal ambition, initiative, and anything else that might disturb Confucian harmony was taboo.

One important aspect of the cultural programming of common people was the concept of *chongjung* (chohng-juung), which refers to paying deferential honor to superiors. In this case, superiors included parents, especially fathers, senior members of the family, elders in general, government authorities, and various spirits and gods.

While modern-day South Koreans are generally more respectful than Westerners toward the same categories of people, nowadays any respect they show is by personal choice, not by government edict or custom.

In fact, after more than 5,000 years of having to keep quiet and take anything their superiors and government wanted to dish out, South Koreans now speak up for their rights and are as quick as any other nationality to take action when they feel they are being wronged.

South Koreans today draw their self-esteem from their education, skills, experience, and overall ability to succeed in a dynamic society—not from being obedient drones.

In this regard, foreigners who are in positions to measure the qualifications of Koreans, for employment or whatever, should be wary of basing their judgment on whether or not the individuals speak English.

While most young South Koreans are becoming bilingual, there are many exceptionally talented older people in the country who speak little or no English, and who make better employees than English speakers.

The Social Pecking Order

There is a specific pecking order between all South Koreans, and until this order is established and recognized there can be very little interaction or harmony. Every new employee introduced into a South Korean group immediately begins steps to find his or her place in the hierarchy. They cannot rest until this is done.

This social pecking order can cause serious problems to the foreign manager who is not aware of it or plays it down. It often happens that the newly arrived Westerner will hire someone for a managerial position simply because he speaks English or has relevant technical knowledge, without considering his educational background or the other things that determine his social position in South Korean society. The foreigner may then hire other people who have a higher social status to work under this manager.

The friction that is likely to result from this situation can seriously affect the operation of the whole company. Experienced expatriates in South Korea avoid this problem by determining the social status of prospective employees themselves, or relying on the input of senior Korean advisors who know how the system works and how to pick the right person for the right job.

The Faction Syndrome

People raised in the Confucian sphere of Asia have a natural propensity to form factions, in whatever group or situation they are in—a response, no doubt, to the fact that behavior in Confucian societies is based on situational ethics—not logic or humane principles that treats everyone equally.

Not surprisingly, *p'a* (ppah), or factions, have been endemic in Korea—historically known as the most Confucian of all Asian nations. Since ancient times, in Korea factions have sprang up in virtually every group made up of more than five or six people, coalescing around the strongest or most charismatic individual on the basis of blood ties, social class, age, birthplace, school ties, and finally common goals.

Virtually all organizations in South Korea, including commercial enterprises, political parties and social groups, are rife with factions. The influence of factions in political circles is visible for all to see—and feel. In commercial enterprises factional influence is generally subtle and may require a finally tuned antenna to detect and keep track of.

However, the larger and stronger a faction in a commercial company, the more likely its members will make less effort to stay under cover—and the greater the likelihood that they will use their weight to get what they want.

It can be especially important for foreign managers in South Korea to be aware of any factions in their enterprises because the *p'a* may be working at cross-purposes with the policies and goals of the management.

This is the kind of intelligence that may come from a variety of sources, including outside consultants, customers, suppliers, and bankers to employees who are not a member of any faction, or are disgruntled with one of them, and for whatever reason decide to inform the foreign managers.

Corporations as Military Units

Unlike their neighbors, South Koreans have never had a warrior mentality, even though the various historical kingdoms maintained armed forces, and occasionally warred against each other. Most of these "clan wars" resulted when a particular regime, usually over a period of several hundred years, became so corrupt the people could no longer stand it, and rose up in rebellion.

But there has long been a military aspect to the Korean mindset as a result of the Confucian principles of rigid organization and discipline that prevailed for generations. This mindset is very conspicuous in the organization and management of South Korean companies, particularly large ones.

In fact, one of the best ways to view and deal with a South Korean corporation is to regard it like a U.S. Marine division, with privates, corporals, sergeants, and officers, whose lives are controlled by rank and a precise protocol.

During the decades of South Korea's rapid economic growth, from the 1960s to the 1990s, the South Korean government itself was controlled by ex-generals, and the country was basically administered more or less as a huge army.

The fact that all male South Koreans in good health are required to spend two to three years in military service when they are between the ages of 20 and 25 continues to condition South Korean men to military discipline and to approach their goals in life with the dedication of a soldier.

The militaristic aspects of the character of South Korean companies and South Korean men naturally impacts on their relationships with foreign companies and foreign businesspeople, and must be taken into account when dealing with them.

The Rank-Based Society

Like their military counterparts, South Koreans are especially sensitive to *chiwi* (chee-wee), or "rank," and it is very important for foreign businesspeople and others to be aware of this cultural factor, and to use it properly in establishing and sustaining goodwill and good working relationships in South Korea. The rank-consciousness of Koreans has a very long history, going back to the emergence of the first clans, and then further institutionalized and ritualized by the infusion of Confucian principles some 2,000 years ago, and continues today.

You might say that Koreans love titles and the pomp and pageantry that is associated with high rank, because for many generations the only people who counted were those with titles. Titles were a major power symbol, and it was necessary to treat those with titles with extraordinary respect.

Foreign businesspeople who want to improve their chances of developing and keeping good relations with South Koreans should make a point of learning their titles and thereafter using them, with and without the names of the individuals.

The rationale for using titles in addressing South Korean businesspeople goes well beyond adhering to deeply entrenched etiquette. Over half of all Koreans share just six family names. In a small office as many as half, if not more, of the staff, may have the same family name.

Fortunately for foreigners who do not speak Korean and have difficulty remembering titles, it is becoming more and more acceptable to address most people with the English titles of Miss, Mrs, and Mr. However, if the individual concerned has a doctorate, it would be a serious blunder to address him or her as Miss, Mrs, or Mr. Doctor, or *paksa* (pahk-sah), the title used for anyone with a Ph.D., should be used.

Rank has its Privileges

Koreans have been conditioned for centuries to exist in a hierarchical society divided from top to bottom into carefully prescribed ranks, with each rank having specific kinds of acceptable behavior. This system has been greatly diluted in recent decades but is still of vital importance in the lives of South Koreans and to foreigners who do business with South Koreans.

In addition to prescribed rules of etiquette within social classes, there is a prescribed form of behavior that is acceptable between the classes. Generally speaking, people in the upper classes prefer to avoid direct contact with those who are two or three grades below them or lower, to ensure their own status is not lowered.

Business executives, in particular, are sensitive about their titles and rank, and go to relative extremes to maintain their positions. They take special care not to lower their own status or raise the level of someone below them by dealing with them as equals. Foreign businessmen, not being members of South Korean society, are normally given the "honorary" status of members of the upper-middle class. Their rank in their company and the rank and image of their company are the next most important factors in their status in South Korea.

As expected, the higher their titles and the larger and better-known their companies, the more prestige they enjoy. Because of the importance of social position and rank, and the necessity of knowing and following the etiquette that is appropriate for each level, South Koreans are obliged to determine these factors as quickly as possible when they meet someone new.

The foreign businessman newly arrived in South Korea can greatly speed up the process of getting acquainted and establishing proper relations with his Korean counterparts, government officials, and others by including his pedigree (i.e., important details about the size of his company if it is not well known, the college or university he attended, any upper-class Korean friends or contacts he might have) in his introduction of himself.

The Military Factor in Business

The military is a conspicuous aspect of life in South Korea, with significant influence in politics, education, private industry, and society in general, just as it was during the country's long feudal dynasties.

Because of the ongoing threat from Communist North Korea, the Republic of Korea (ROK) has been on a high military alert status since the ending of the Korean War in 1953. All eligible males must register for the draft and, with few exceptions, undergo military training and spend time in the reserves. Government regulations about military service are rigorously enforced. The government will not hire adult males who have not completed their military training. They may also be denied the right to obtain a passport and travel abroad.

The military training system is very thorough and tough, with a strict discipline that later carries over into civilian life. There is great prestige in being selected for schooling at a military academy and going on to a career as a military officer. Those who succeed in reaching the higher ranks are invariably assured equally prestigious positions in government or within private industry after they retire.

Most foreign businesses in the ROK accommodate themselves to this situation and attempt to see the positive side. Generally speaking, the foreign business community supports the position of the government that North Korea poses a direct military threat to the ROK. There is also a general consensus that the militaristic bent of South Koreans has been a major contributing factor in the economic advances made by South Korea since the 1960s. The reference here, of course, is to the fact that South Korean companies and the various government agencies marshal and manage their manpower very much like military organizations, and plot their strategy and tactics with the precision and purpose that is characteristic of military campaigns. They also demand the same kind of loyalty, commitment, and sacrifices that are typical of the military in do-or-die situations.

Cold Calls Are Out

In earlier decades, Western businessmen visiting South Korea could ignore etiquette and make cold calls to South Korean companies—first because South Koreans were exceedingly anxious to make contact with foreign companies and would compromise their own ethics, and second because of a strong desire to be accommodating and hospitable to visiting foreigners.

Times have changed, especially when it comes to large corporations. Foreigners who visit these companies without appointments may be received politely, but not necessarily by the one they want to see. It is now very important, if not absolutely essential, that you make an appointment with the individual you want to meet.

If you want to make any progress in developing a relationship it is also vital that you make sure the individual concerned has received well in advance a substantial amount of information about your company and yourself.

There are, of course, exceptions to these general rules and customs. Younger South Korean managers and executives who have been educated abroad and absorbed Western business etiquette can often be reached by email or phone, and may agree to an appointment on short notice.

Appointments and Meetings

The pace of business in South Korea might be equated with a dead run, and the higher ranking the manager or executive, the busier their schedules. Promptness is essential.

The best times for business meetings are usually 10:00 a.m. to 12:00 p.m. and 2:00 p.m. to 3:00 p.m. Business dinners are common. Midday meetings also take place in hotel coffee shops and restaurants. Business breakfasts are becoming common among the international crowd.

South Korean businesspeople generally take their vacations from mid-July to mid-August. Other inconvenient appointment times include early October, a time of many holidays, and Christmas time. Typical business hours are 9:00 a.m. to 5:00 p.m. Monday through Friday, and 9 a.m. to 1 p.m. on Saturday.

When entering a group meeting, the senior member of a party typically enters the conference room first, followed by the next highest ranking person, and so on. When greeting business contingents, South Koreans line up in the order of their rank.

Office Call Protocol

Office calls should be treated as formal affairs, especially if you are visiting a company for the first time. It is not only polite but expeditious to make the appointment well in advance and advise the people you want to see what you want to talk about. South Koreans are reluctant to say "no" directly and do not like to appear uncooperative or unresponsive, with the result that the inexperienced foreign businessman can waste a lot of time making presentations to a company that has absolutely no interest in his idea or project because they may not come out and say so.

One approach is to write to the company well in advance, providing as many details as possible about your project, thereby giving the appropriate people in the company time to discuss your proposal and at least make a preliminary decision about whether or not they want to pursue it. Companies with no interest in your project will generally eliminate themselves with a written response or by not responding at all. Another approach—often the best one—is to enlist the aid of a local go-between or consultant who can sound out the company on your behalf.

A significant percentage of all new business relationships in South Korea begin with personal connections. The first step in the approach to a company is an attempt to line up these personal contacts. At present, high-level government officials are among the most effective contacts the businessman in South Korea can have. If you can get the personal backing of an important ministry official it will open many business doors.

At the same time, South Koreans, including government bureaucrats, often do not dispense favors without expecting something in return. This something can range from an enhancement of their image to an indirect participation in the venture being proposed. These matters are usually very subtle, and often require the sensitive antennae of an experienced South Korean to properly execute—particularly so if you cannot communicate fluently with the official concerned.

If you do bring in a local consultant or agent, you have, of course, added another layer to whatever relationship might develop between you and your target company.

Dressing for Business

During Korea's long feudal era under the Choson dynasty, the materials, style, and quality of the clothing worn by the people was determined by the government and was based on class and occupation. This custom made all Koreans extraordinarily sensitive to wearing apparel, and its influence continues to be conspicuously discernible in present-day South Korea. Conservative suits, shirts, and ties are so much a part of the persona of South Korean businessmen that one wag noted that all male Koreans were born already dressed in three-piece suits. The conservatism that has long distinguished the dress of South Korean office workers is not as strict as it was in the 1990s, but on average they are more sedate than their Western counterparts.

This does not mean that Western businessmen should follow suit—but overly loud suits, shirts, and ties are taken as a lack of cultural refinement, and therefore do not reflect well on the wearer.

Office women in South Korea are as stylish, if not more so, than their most sophisticated counterparts in London, New York, Paris, or Tokyo—but on the conservative side as far as colors and cut are concerned. Blouses and skirts are the norm but pants and pantsuits for women are gradually gaining acceptance.

Sleeveless tops and miniskirts remain taboo in business settings. In many homes and restaurants diners sit on the floor at low tables, making both mini-skirts and tight skirts incompatible.

The Dual Role of Name Cards

Name cards are a vital part of doing business in South Korea, not only as a means of identifying individuals by their companies and positions, but also to help distinguish between the vast number of people in the country who have the same last name.

In addition to their practical use in identifying individuals, name cards also play a significant role in helping to establish the social status of each individual, and subsequently the level of language and other etiquette that is an integral part of the social system.

The formal way to present a name card is with both hands and a slight bow, giving your name at the same time. As the power of old etiquette weakens and people become more informal in their behavior, presenting a card with the right hand is becoming common. However, using the left hand to present a card, or anything else, remains impolite.

Name cards should be bilingual, not only because it is the professional thing to do but also as a courtesy to demonstrate respect for South Korea and South Korean culture, and as a sign that the individual is serious about doing business in South Korea.

Visiting businesspeople should, of course, make sure they are well supplied with bilingual name cards, as it is common to go through fifty or more in one day.

If you are seated at a table when you receive someone's card, it is both customary and practical to lay it on the table in front of you so you can read the name and title during the following conversation.

Writing on someone's business card while still in their presence is still considered a no-no by some, but you can certainly do it later to help you recall the individual.

The Use of First Names

The use of first names is still not common among South Korean businesspeople and adults in general. (At one time in South Korean history one's first name was kept secret. Even saying it out loud was taboo.)

Foreign businesspeople who have developed close, personal relationships with their South Korean counterparts and use their first names in information situations should never address them by their first names at meetings or in other formal situations.

When speaking in English, the accepted practice in addressing people in business is to use the common Western prefixes, Mr, Mrs, or Miss. It is also good etiquette for foreigners to use the English equivalents of the titles of ranking businesspeople and other professionals.

Gift Giving vs. Bribery

In the Confucian sphere of Asia, gift-giving has traditionally been one of the foundations of establishing and sustaining relationships with individuals who are important in one's life—from teachers and doctors to employers, customers, suppliers, and government officials.

Part of this custom evolved from the fact that in ancient times it became customary to present gifts of food, drink, and other valuables to gods and other deities to win and keep their goodwill and protection. Until money was invented, giving chiefs, priests, and others something in kind was a way of paying them as well as getting their support and/or protection. Government officials in feudal Korea had the power of life and death, so giving them *sonmul* (sohn-muhl), or gifts, became a matter of survival. Such tributes and gifts were not regarded as immoral. They were the "oil" that allowed the societies to function smoothly. Where common people were concerned, giving gifts to officials was often the only way they could get the help or services they needed.

Not surprisingly, the bounds of propriety were often exceeded, especially by well-to-do upper class people, who gave gifts to officials to repay obligations and when seeking new favors. Giving gifts in the form of tribute, primarily for protection, was also a traditional custom. From 108 B.C. to A.D. 1910, the various kingdoms on the Korean peninsula paid an annual tribute to China as a way of maintaining their independence.

During the long Choson era (1392–1910), the gift-giving custom was sorely abused by government officials and others in power, who demanded what amounted to *noemul* (noh-muhl), or bribes, for their services, in the guise of gifts.

Both legitimate gift-giving and out-and-out bribery became even more scandalous during South Korea's build up to economic prominence from 1960 onwards. In the early 1990s, the government finally instituted precise guidelines for giving gifts in an effort to cut down on the corruption that had become endemic among government officials.

These new laws reduced but did not stop the practice of bribery in the form of gifts, and ensuing scandals engulfed even government officials at the highest levels, with two former presidents arrested and sentenced for accepting bribes. It is now illegal to give gifts of any significance to government officials, and efforts to eliminate the practice have become stronger and more effective over the years.

Foreigners doing business in South Korea should exercise great care to not get caught up in any gift or favor giving action that might be construed as *noemul*. Small, personal gifts among business friends are perfectly legal and much appreciated by Koreans.

Foreign companies operating in South Korea should have an anti-*noemul* statement in their corporate constitution. But occasions may still arise in which some form of "gift-giving" is the only solution to a problem. In which case, the only recourse may be to get input from a senior, trusted South Korean advisor on how to handle the situation.

Gift giving remains an established ritual in South Korea, playing a key role in creating and sustaining relationships, both in business situations and on all levels of society.

Chon jimina (choan jee-me-nah), which translates, more or less, as "one centimeter of feelings," refers to the small gifts that Korean businessmen customarily give to people they meet during the course of a trip, to show appreciation and express thanks for relatively small favors. It is a good practice for foreign businessmen to emulate on their trips to South Korea.

When returning home from overseas trips, South Korean businesspeople bring gifts for their families and close work associates. It is also common for them to buy locally famous products as gifts when they travel in South Korea.

To Bow or Not to Bow?

All ancient people apparently bowed down to superiors and symbols of power to demonstrate respect, but the Chinese went much further. They institutionalized and ritualized the bow, making it the formal, official style of social interaction, from greetings and farewells, to apologies, petitions, praying, and so on.

This universalized version of the *chol* (choll), or bow, was introduced into Korea in 109 B.C. by the Chinese when they invaded the peninsula and more or less administered it as a province for the next 400 years. Later Korean dynasties embellished the *chol* in a variety of ways, including the choice of language used for different occasions.

All of the guidebooks on doing business in South Korea cover the role and importance of the *chol* in South Korean society. The bow is still the official, formal method of greeting and leave-taking in South Korea, and there are numerous occasions when it is also appropriate behavior for Westerners—such as at formal functions, and when greeting older men and women who have not adopted Western ways.

But the Western handshake has been integrated into modern South Korean society and is used when dealing with foreigners. An increasing number of South Koreans of all ages now use the handshake among themselves on all but official and formal occasions.

Where foreigners are concerned, the occasion and people involved generally dictates whether one should bow or shake hands. Koreans are not bashful or reticent about sticking out their hand for a shake, so usually all the foreigner has to do is respond in kind.

Whether or not one should shake hands with a South Korean is generally not a problem. Koreans are traditionally a friendly, ebullient people and, unlike many other Asians, often make the first move to greet a guest or new acquaintance with a good, strong handshake. Like some Latinos and Europeans, South Koreans will often use both hands when they want to emphasize their goodwill, friendship, or gratitude to someone.

Where bowing is concerned, there are several different kinds or grades of Korean bows, depending on the age and rank or social position of the individuals involved, as well as on the circumstances of the bowing. The higher the individual, the more shallow his or her bow. Lower-ranking individuals, and those expressing especially deep or sincere thanks, execute deeper bows. People seeking favors or apologizing bow lower than normal to emphasize the point.

South Koreans who are used to meeting and working with foreigners generally shake hands instead of bowing. The bow is not a casual gesture among South Koreans. It is a very direct and conspicuous indication of their relative status, which is jealously guarded, and must therefore be performed properly to avoid giving serious offense.

When South Korean businesspeople meet for the first time they do not know how to bow to each other until their relative status is established. The first thing they usually do is exchange name cards. If this is not sufficient to clearly establish a hierarchical relationship, they may diplomatically inquire about each other's ages, schools, and families.

There is a tendency for foreigners who have been in South Korea for a long time to subconsciously pick up the habit of bowing, although they generally do not utilize the deep bow. They invariably learn at the same time when it is proper to bow, when a bow can be combined with a handshake, and when to only shake hands.

Newcomers who are in doubt about which is appropriate are usually safe if they combine a modest bow and a handshake with everyone, except older women who have not been exposed to Westernization. One should bow to them.

Standing Up at the Right Time

It is common practice for South Korean businessmen to indicate respect for visitors to their offices by standing up. It is also regarded as impolite for lower-ranking employees to remain seated while their superior stands. This custom is reinforced by the fact that all young South Korean men are required to serve a period of time in the military, where they are drilled in showing proper respect to superiors and guests, including standing up when a superior arrives on the scene.

Higher-level South Korean businessmen may not stand up when someone they do not know arrives, and this is particularly so in the case of government officials, unless informed that the visitor outranks them or is a special guest. Businessmen and government officials may remain seated if they do not particularly want to see the visitor or do not like the visitor for any reason.

Until recent decades, women in Korea had virtually no status and were required to defer to men in virtually all circumstances. While this has changed considerably, men still take precedence over women in most common situations, where Western chivalry or courtesy would put women first. Western businessmen who demonstrate unusual courtesy to South Korean women in the presence of un-Westernized South Korean men may embarrass both the women and the men. The best approach in this situation is to extend basic courtesy without making a show of it.

In rural areas, as well as in the most traditional homes and companies in the cities, women still take a backseat to men.

Rounds of Greetings

One of the key aspects of business relationships in South Korea comes under the heading of *insa* (een-sah), which means "round of greetings." In addition to referring to the typical greetings between people on informal and social occasions, *insa* also relates to a formal obligation that businesspeople, and people in general, have to visit and greet friends, work superiors, business and government contacts, and others who play a role in their lives.

The *insa* plays a special role in social and business affairs in South Korea, because it establishes the relative social position and rank of the individuals concerned, and reaffirms personal relations. Businessmen regularly visit their key contacts to greet them formally as a way of sustaining their network of connections. A written greeting is an *insa jang*.

On the personal side, there are a number of occasions when *insa* visits are required, including a death in the family, marriages, major holidays, and other significant events in the lives of people.

On the business front, *insa* visits to contacts in other companies and government agencies, customers, and suppliers, are generally made a number of times a year. The more important the contact, the more often *insa* visits are needed. Occasions for such visits include the beginning of new projects, when an important contact gets promoted, and so on.

The most important *insa* visits occur at the close of each year, beginning around December 15th, and at the beginning of each new year, between January 3rd and 5th. End of the year visits are aimed at expressing appreciation to clients, customers, and suppliers for their business during the year, and to request to continue the relationship during the coming year.

Insa visits immediately following New Year's are even more important. These visits are referred to as *sebae* (say-bay), which literally means "beginning of the year bow" but is usually translated as "New Year's greeting." These are courtesy calls that people make on senior managers, directors, and presidents of the companies they do business with.

The aim of the *sebae* visits is obvious—to nurture ongoing good personal relationships with key individuals to help ensure that the successful business relationships with their firms or agencies will continue.

Sebae visits are generally more ceremonial than end-of-the year visits and other *insa* visits during the year, with the visitors formally expressing thanks for past business and their sincere wishes for the continuation of the relationship during the coming new year. These visits, which usually last for only a few minutes because there is often a stream of visitors calling on larger companies and more important government offices, normally include drinking toasts to each other. The events are thus festive in nature, and by midday nobody is feeling any pain.

South Korean companies stage their own *shimushik* (sheem-uu-sheek), or "starting business ceremony" on the first business day of the new year. These ceremonies include eating a number of special foods, drinking, and lots of speeches by company executives and managers.

Foreign businesspeople working in South Korea are well advised to follow both the *insa* and *sebae* customs.

Another custom among South Korea's large corporations that foreigners need to be aware of, and to emulate when the occasion arises, is known as *songbyul hoe* (sohng-buhl hoe-eh), which means "farewell party." This is a party thrown by a section or division when a member is being sent abroad on an overseas assignment. Farewell parties are noted for numerous speeches, lots of good food, and enthusiastic toasting, but they are designed to do more than just provide employees with a good time at company expense. They are a way of instilling loyalty and bonding the employees.

The South Korean View and Use of Contracts

The Western-style contract is still relatively new to South Korea. There were business arrangements of all kinds during Korea's long feudal era, many of them in writing, but they were simple agreements and documents that left the details and implementation of the contracts open so they could evolve with the changing circumstances. As in many old societies, "gentlemen's agreements" were the rule.

The emotional and friendship aspects of agreements were what made them binding. The Korean perspective was that as long as the parties to an agreement were sincere and honorable it would be fulfilled, regardless of any unforeseen circumstances.

The Korean word for a Western-style contract is *kyeyak* (keh-yahk), and both the word and such contracts are now common in international business relationships. But in the eyes of South Koreans, a written contract is little more than a piece of paper if the parties to it are not trustworthy.

Broadly speaking, when South Koreans sign contracts with their foreign counterparts it is more of a formality indicating that they have a relationship with someone—as opposed to being an agreement that is cast in stone and to which they must abide no matter what happens. One South Korean businessman said: "We regard contracts as general guidelines that set perimeters around which we will work."

Traditional South Koreans say their own *kyeyak* originate from the philosophical foundation of *injong* (een-johng), or "compassion for the plight of others." They usually add, or imply, that *injong* is typically missing from Western contracts.

The already large and growing cadre of South Korean business-people who were educated abroad and/or spent years in overseas assignments are generally at home and at ease with Western-style contracts, and when problems do develop among their stay-at-home colleagues they can usually resolve the situation to everyone's satisfaction.

When South Koreans sign a Western contract they are putting their "face," and often their fate in their companies, on the line, so it is a very serious matter. The more "face" they have to lose, the more likely they will adhere strictly to the contract.

While making sure that their own interests are protected, foreign businesspeople seeking to contract with South Koreans obviously should bring in expert legal and cultural advisors to help make sure the contracts are acceptable to the South Koreans in both a business and cultural context.

Once large-scale contracts are worked out and signed, foreigners should follow South Korean custom and mark the occasion with a celebration that includes drinks and speeches. These events traditionally end with all of the participants simultaneously raising their arms in the air and shouting, *Mansei!* (mahn-say-ee!), which literally means "Ten thousand years!" and is the South Korean equivalent of "Hip! Hip! Hooray!"

Baek ji wiim (bake jee weem), literally "trusting in white paper," is a term often used to infer that someone is doing business on the basis of nothing more solid or permanent than a piece of paper with a signature on it—which is a pretty good description of a contract. The concept derives from the fact that South Koreans believe a deep personal relationship is the only proper foundation for a business deal.

Still today, the basic South Korean concept of a contract, particularly the view of government bureaucrats, differs fundamentally from the way Westerners view and use them. The typical foreign view is that once you negotiate an agreement and sign a contract, that's it—the relationship proceeds forward on mutually acceptable, solid ground.

That is not the case at all in South Korea. The signing of the contract is usually when trouble begins, because from the very beginning the contract is interpreted one way by the South Korean side and another way by the foreign party. Generally speaking, South Koreans sign contracts with foreign businessmen to get the relationship officially moving.

Thereafter everything is subject to change and negotiation. South Koreans do not regard the provisions of contracts as written in stone or as the fundamental basis of a business relationship. They regard the personal relationship and the desire for mutual benefits as the foundation of any business arrangement. A contract is essentially nothing more than a symbol of this relationship.

In the context of South Korean thought, contractual obligations must change in the same way that business conditions and political situations change, in order for the relationship to be kept current—from their viewpoint, of course.

Being personal agreements rather than immutable laws, the terms of a particular contract go out the door when the signatories or the managers of a contract change. From this point, any contract is subject to the interpretations and expectations of the new managers, who devise a new set of unwritten terms to govern the relationship with the second party—and often implement these changes without informing the other side.

This is a vital difference in the concept of a contract that the foreign businessman must understand in order to do business in South Korea. The essence is that when a South Korean executive signs a contract with a foreign company, he is not necessarily obligating his own corporation to uphold the provisions of that contract. The corporation may not accept the obligation if it has a good reason to do so. It may be regarded as a personal matter between the managers who negotiated and signed the contract and the foreign party.

The sanctity of contracts is even less assured where government officials are concerned. Not being direct parties to the agreement, they have no qualms about declaring any contract they do not like as no longer appropriate and needing renegotiation (so as to be more favorable to the South Korean side), or null and void, eliminating the responsibility of the South Korean altogether.

Since government bureaucrats are shifted around regularly, often on an annual basis, contracts between South Korean and foreign businessmen often coming up for review by people who know nothing at all about the original negotiation but who have the power to require that they be altered or scrapped. Incoming bureaucrats frequently feel compelled to demonstrate their efficiency and patriotism by questioning relationships between South Korean and foreign companies and ordering significant changes in their contractual arrangements.

Not all the contractual problems between South Korean and Western companies are on the South Korean side. Western companies frequently play musical chairs with their top personnel in South Korea, breaking the personal relationships that foreign managers have established with their Korean counterparts, and making it necessary for their replacements to virtually start over in developing new ties for their companies. If these transitions are not handled thoughtfully and carefully over a period of time (and many of them are not), the switch in personnel gives the Korean side an opening to make unilateral, fundamental changes in the terms of the relationship.

It is especially important for any contract with a South Korean company to be as clear, as comprehensive, and yet as flexible as possible. A major challenge is to anticipate changes that are likely to occur that would affect the operation of the agreement, and to make sure they are covered in the contract. Again, a shift in managers involved in implementing a contract can often affect its status.

Basically, the contract represents the intentions and understandings of the two participants at the time of signing, and if these are clear and complete, you are off to the best possible start. One problem is making sure that both sides do indeed understand what the other means, and are in fact agreeing to that. This may entail a great deal of extra effort in bridging the cultural differences, overcoming communications problems, and really getting down to the "facts" of the deal.

There is always the possibility that both sides will agree to things they really do not like just to get the contract signed, while intending to negotiate further later. This especially applies to South Korean companies. It behooves the foreign participant to make a special, patient effort to draw out the true feelings and intentions of the Korean partners right from the very beginning, to ensure they sign a contract that is to everyone's satisfaction.

Once a contract is signed, it is important to maintain an ongoing dialogue with your Korean counterparts to keep updated on their thinking and to make the adjustments invariably necessary to keep the relationship steady. This is often the area in which the Western partner fails, because it requires a conscious commitment that is time- and energy-consuming (and often costly)—to adequately nurture the relationship.

The South Korean government has attempted to address the differing cultural view of contracts by creating "model" contracts for licensing technology and other business arrangements. Both parties to such contracts must be assured that the written obligations are fully understood.

Big Foreign Company Myopia

It seems that the bigger the foreign company, the more likely it is to get into trouble in South Korea in both negotiating and nurturing contracts. One typical classic example involved Chrysler's famous Lee Iacocca and his top people, who came to Seoul several times, made no effort at all to take advantage of the accumulated experience and wisdom of the American Chamber of Commerce in South Korea (AmCham) in Seoul, and wasted a lot of time and money.

The Chrysler people spent a lot of time trying to talk Samsung, the electronics manufacturer, into going into producing automobiles. There were already four automobile manufacturers in South Korea at that time and there was no way the government was going to let a fifth company enter the field. Samsung wouldn't let on that what Chrysler wanted was impossible because it hoped the government would make an exception of its policy and let them do it. Chrysler is said to have spent millions before they gave up, and instead went with Hyundai.

If the Chrysler people had had the common sense to visit AmCham they could have learned this lesson for nothing, and saved a great deal of time, frustration, and ill will. "It was incredible that they didn't talk to a single person in Seoul to get advice or help," said a local businessman.

Eventually, of course, Chrysler did work out an agreement with Samsung to provide them with auto parts, but it was a very long and expensive way of developing the relationship.

Since then, a number of other American companies have gotten themselves into situations in which they were pitting their reputation and style against the South Korean government or against the Korean way of doing things. That is a no-win situation and should be avoided.

Major Problem Areas

Working-level employees in South Korea's government agencies and ministries do not always approve of policies advocated and announced by senior ministry officials. They have the power to delay or stop completely any application that comes to them, and sometimes do so without any apparent reason for their actions.

There are also many "unpublished rules" regarding the government's approval process in any new venture. The applicant too often finds out about these internal guidelines, working rules, and regulations only after applying for approval of a project. Of course, this problem can be greatly reduced if the foreign businessman enlists the advice of attorneys and consultants in Seoul who specialize in dealing with the appropriate government offices.

Lower-level civil servants who are responsible for the administration of the laws governing foreign investment and operation often have little if any international experience, resulting in communication problems, delays, and sometimes serious misunderstandings. The best approach in this situation is to be very patient and helpful, and to maintain a very humble attitude to avoid rubbing the officials the wrong way.

Dealing through an experienced troubleshooter, who usually already knows the officials and can anticipate their reactions and needs, can also, of course, be of significant help.

Another problem facing foreign companies in South Korea are the extraordinary demands made by the government and numerous associations and charities on foreign companies for donations. While such donations are ostensibly voluntary, when the request comes from an official in a powerful agency or ministry it can be difficult—and may be unwise—to refuse.

Here again, a very astute, local go-between who has a wide network of contacts is often needed to advise the foreign businessman when he can safely ignore an unreasonable request for a donation.

AmCham members agree that one of the main challenges facing a foreign company wanting to establish a joint-venture operation in South Korea is selecting the best possible partner. It used to be that members of the large business/industrial combines, the *chaebols*, generally made the best joint-venture partners because of the influence they had with government ministries. Now there are occasions when it can be a handicap instead of a help to join up with a *chaebol* because the government's policy is to favor medium-sized and smaller firms over the giants.

Another surprising problem in tying up with one of the more successful South Korean corporations is that making huge profits is still basically regarded as immoral in the context of South Korean values, so any foreign company that aligns itself with a South Korean company that is conspicuous for its profits is liable to fall victim to some of the local opprobrium felt toward the South Korean partner.

Finally, the bigger and more successful the South Korean partner, the more likely it is to insist on running the joint venture its way, regardless of what the foreign partner thinks is best. This may work fine as long as the policies and practices of the South Korean partner result in the kind of success the foreign partner is seeking. When it doesn't work out that way, the foreign partner has very little recourse.

Conflicting Goals

Joint-venture operations in South Korea are subject to a great many clearly defined cultural strains that put an exceptional burden on the foreign side. One of the most important of these potential problem areas is a basic conflict between the goals of the two parties. The primary purpose of the foreign partner is to make a profit and remit dividends outside of South Korea. The chief aim of the South Korean partner is generally to realize company growth and make an overall contribution to the South Korean economy and society at large.

Since both of these positions are virtually absolute, the only sensible recourse is for the foreign partner to be very much aware of this fundamental conflict, discuss it at length during the early stages of the formation of the joint venture, and attempt to reach a mutually acceptable agreement in writing when handling this important part of the relationship.

Playing Games with the Books

There is a strong tendency for South Korean companies, especially those sponsored by the government, to use "flexible" accounting practices to avoid showing a loss at the end of the year. The main reason for this creative bookkeeping where government-sponsored enterprises are concerned is to prevent the ministry involved from investigating the company and possibly closing it down, replacing the management, or publicly criticizing the management, which would harm the image of the company as well as the individual executives.

When this happens in privately-owned companies, it is generally to make the company look in better shape, to save face, and to avoid loss of confidence on the part of suppliers or customers. The foreign businessman looking for an agent or partner in South Korea is cautioned to do a thorough financial check before making any final decisions. Otherwise what you see may not be what you get.

Privacy South Korean Style

The concept of privacy within a company is very weak in South Korea. South Koreans tend to assume that any matter or information that concerns the company also concerns them, and it is difficult to keep anything confidential or limited to the knowledge of an individual. Attempts to keep things from employees of a company are likely to be regarded as signs of distrust or arrogance.

This often calls for deft diplomacy in dealing with managers and others on an internal as well as an external basis. It is especially important to avoid appearing unfair to any individual, which includes upsetting his sense of status in relation to his coworkers. There is generally no problem in protecting company confidentiality as far as outsiders are concerned, and South Koreans are very sensitive about their own privacy outside the company.

There have been instances in the past of secretaries of foreign business managers in South Korea gathering up the company files and taking them to a South Korean company to be copied. The moral of this story is that foreign managers should take every measure possible to ensure that their secretaries are loyal.

Working for a Boss, Not a Company

It has often been said of South Koreans that, unlike the Japanese, they work for a boss instead of a company. The inference is that South Koreans identify themselves intimately with the individuals they work for because it is more natural and easier for them to be loyal to an individual than to a faceless company. This means that the relationship between managers and employees is of vital importance. It also means that the foreign employer or boss in South Korea must bear the responsibility of establishing and maintaining a relationship of integrity and trust between himself and his South Korean employees.

It is also noted that honor and integrity among South Koreans tends to be reserved for those they know, respect, trust, and have an ongoing relationship with. If these conditions do not exist, South Koreans may readily sign a contract they know they are not going to keep, and take whatever advantage presents itself.

Female Employees

The long-standing Korean tradition of men and women living in separate worlds in their personal lives, as well as work, was an important factor in the hiring and use of female employees until the late 1900s. Because of the lingering Confucian attitudes of the past, there was a large pool of well-educated, talented young South Korean women who could not find jobs in South Korean companies that befitted their education, knowledge, and ambitions.

Many of these young women found employment with foreign companies, where their extraordinary energy, goodwill, and talents were welcomed. There has since been a growing number of companies founded by women and primarily managed by women—some of them extraordinarily successful.

As noted, the traditional male attitudes towards women in South Korea have, in fact, changed to the point that in 2013 a woman was elected president of the country. Women have made up a significant proportion of the labor force since the 1970s.

Foreign-educated Korean women who have become bicultural and bilingual are prize employees for foreign companies.

Women and Male Chauvinism

The pressure for South Korean wives to have sons took a frightening turn in the 1970s when the amniotic fluid test used to determine the sex of unborn children was introduced. Abortions of female fetuses rose dramatically. In 1980 a more accurate and inexpensive method was introduced, and the number of abortions went even higher.

Mothers-in-law were said to be responsible for the sex tests and the decisions for aborting so many female fetuses. Male chauvinism is still a potent force in the lives of all South Koreans, but South Korean women are not passive vassals content to be the playthings of men. Not by any measure. Virtually every foreigner with any experience in South Korea will tell you that South Korean women are stronger than the men, cleverer than the men, more dependable, and more diplomatic (the latter because whatever they do publicly, it has to make the men look good).

Until the late 1990s there were few South Korean women in management or other positions of public power. Those few who were in positions in which they managed males, no matter how low the level of activity, had to be very careful not to upset the ego of the men. Often, the power of the females came from a high social position rather than from an occupational or professional position.

But as women gained more personal economic security and free time, they began going after what they wanted with extraordinary passion. "They were pulling themselves up by their girdle-straps," said one veteran foreign resident and successful businesswoman in South Korea.

As part of their concern for "face" and feelings, South Koreans make great use of compliments (*chansa*), but the custom is deeply chauvinistic in that older men do not customarily compliment women. It is advisable for foreign men in South Korea to be aware of this custom when they are tempted to conspicuously praise the looks, dress, or accomplishments of South Korean women in the presence of South Korean men.

The Great Walls of South Korea

There are a number of specific handicaps in doing business in South Korea that derive from the fear of excessive foreign influence and a deep-seated nationalism.

Strong nationalism plays a vital role in the success or failure of foreign companies in South Korea. It is most often expressed in a negative way in regard to official government policies. Lower bureaucrats who believe that a stated government policy is bad for South Korea (or a South Korean company) will go to extraordinary lengths to prevent the policy or the action from being carried out.

Foreign businesspeople must learn how to deal with these problems by utilizing a variety of techniques, from enlisting the aid of influential South Korean advisors or go-betweens to going to extraordinary lengths to develop close personal relationships in the important ministries and agencies.

Another cultural factor that acts as a wall in doing business in South Korea is the inferior-superior structure of South Korean society. The vertical arrangements in all organizations tend to be exclusive and fiercely competitive, making it difficult or impossible for people in these vertical entities to communicate and cooperate with each other. This often results in irrational and irritating delays in any dealings, particularly those involving the government.

Disobeying Laws

South Koreans are still getting used to obeying *pop* (pope), laws, that are designed to control their behavior in a free, democratic society. In earlier times, there were very few laws. Anything that disturbed the prescribed social system, as well as anything that irritated a superior, was wrong—and not detailing them in laws was seen as a way to deter people from doing anything not specifically approved.

Generally speaking, South Koreans still do not like written laws, and do not agree with the principle of legalism, which calls for obeying the letter of the law. They prefer to conduct themselves and to settle differences in human terms, giving precedent to circumstances and human feelings.

Judges who deal only in facts and make decisions on the basis of written laws are regarded as cruel and anti-human, and unfit to be judges. This view of the law can cause problems to foreigners, especially Westerners, who have been raised on the idea that the rule of law takes precedence over everything else.

Foreign businesspeople are thus advised to exhaust all practical and possible means of resolving disputes and other issues with their South Korean counterparts before resorting to the law. Professional go-betweens can often be very helpful in such cases because they bring a more balanced perspective to the issues and are much less likely to unfairly favor the South Korean side.

Reading Each Other's *Nunchi*

Because of the minutely prescribed and structured form of social behavior that prevailed in feudal Korea for generations, the national mindset and etiquette became homogenized to an extraordinary degree—to a point, in fact, that much of the communication became non-verbal. People could anticipate the actions and read the body language of others more or less like an open book.

The process of divining the intentions of others without resorting to words came to be known as *nunchi* (nuun-chee), which translates roughly as "to measure with the eye," or figuratively "to read minds"—something that I have labeled "cultural telepathy."

While South Korean culture is no longer as homogenized as it was before the 1960s, and is getting more varied every day, the traditional mindset and behavioral patterns are still intact enough that they impact directly on all relationships.

Foreigners in South Korea typically encounter situations in which they are expected to divine the intentions of their South Korean friends, coworkers, employees, and others through *nunchi*, rather than detailed, explicit explanations. These situations can range from being mild inconveniences to being very serious problems that become even worse if they are not recognized and addressed.

Dr. C. Paul Dredge, a senior associate of the South Korean Strategy Association, writing in *South Korea Business World*, recounted a typical incident involving the foreign manager of a joint-venture company in Seoul. The firm's office was located in a very expensive but inconvenient location in Yoido, near the

National Assembly Building. The foreign manager found a nice suite of offices in the downtown area of Seoul, less expensive and far more convenient for both employees and visitors.

At the last moment, the South Korean president refused to allow the move to take place, and would not explain his reasons to the foreign manager. The situation developed into a sticky impasse that created a great deal of ill will on both sides.

The foreign manager had explained his reasons for wanting to move the office, and believed his rationale had been understood and accepted by his joint-venture partner. He had therefore proceeded in good faith. The South Korean president had opposed the move from the beginning, however, and had relied upon the foreigner's ability to read his *nunchi* to understand that he was firmly against the move, although he had not said so directly.

The South Korean president preferred the Yoido location because it was one of the most prestigious districts in the city. It gave the company "face" on the highest government and business levels, and, as Dredge observed, "The Yoido location had nothing to do with rent and everything to do with where the company president wanted his car to pull up in the morning."

The president and other South Korean personnel did not simply come out and tell the foreigner that there was no way they were going to move the offices because they did not want to confront him directly with their objections and cause him to lose face in a contest he could not win. They felt it was up to him to ask the right questions and to "read" the right answers. In the end, as Dredge noted, both sides lost face in a classic case of failure in cross-cultural communications.

Added Dredge: "No amount of training in cross-cultural communication can prepare an expatriate manager to conduct the technical aspects of the business of his company in South Korea. But adding cross-cultural sensitivity to his technical and managerial skills and experience puts the manager and his company at a distinct advantage—in discussions of office location, in contract negotiations, in adjustment to family life in Seoul, and in every other aspect of his daily activities, both professional and personal."

Learning how to communicate with South Koreans via *nunchi* is not something that comes easily or quickly. In addition to a good command of the South Korean language, one has to become sensitized to every nuance of the verbal and body languages and know how to interpret them. This means that the average foreign businessperson in South Korea needs to have access to advice from a very loyal, very experienced South Korean to act as his or her "cultural telepathy" interpreter.

Being skilled at *nunchi* is one of the most important business and social assets a person can have, and such people are highly valued because they are the ones who help keep a workplace peaceful and productive.

Of course, this facet of South Korean culture puts foreigners at a decided disadvantage—unless they are bilingual and bicultural. Not being able to tune into the cultural channel that reveals the *kibun* (feelings or real intentions) of South Korean employees, foreigners have to depend on help from others—usually an older, seasoned employee who is genuinely committed to the welfare and success of the individual foreigner and his company.

Fortunately, younger generations of South Koreans, particularly those with international experience, are less sensitive about keeping their *kibun* intact as they become more individualistic and self-assured. The word itself is now heard much less often than in the past, but the feelings it refers to are still a significant part of the South Korean psyche and should not be ignored.

In the past, it has most often been the South Korean businessman who learned the Westerner's ways and made adjustments to accommodate them. The advantages of inter-cultural understanding accrued to him alone. Since the 1970s, however, South Korea's position as an emerging economic power has created a flow of economic activity so dynamic that the cultural accommodation of only one side of the Western-South Korean partnership is no longer sufficient for either side.

Dr. Dredge says that some expatriate managers have grown tired of hearing that things are done differently in South Korea, but "when they and their colleagues put forth the effort necessary to learn the fundamentals of how that is so (or to distinguish between important cultural differences and cases in which citing such differences is little more than a beginning ploy), they can use their knowledge not only to avoid making mistakes, but to gain positive management and negotiating skills."

The Role and Importance of Social Status

Social status remains a vital factor in personal and business relations in South Korea. The foreign businessperson who is going to establish an office or factory in South Korea must be aware of this and take it into account. To employ a South Korean with a low social status as a manager—because of his English language ability, his experience, or any other qualification—and expect him to be able to effectively manage employees with higher social pedigrees will usually result in problems.

Generally speaking, the higher the South Korean is in the managerial hierarchy of a foreign company, the higher his social status should be to avoid undesirable repercussions from other employees. Social class in South Korea is determined by several factors, including ancestry, schools attended, where the individual was born, and where the person presently lives. The social elite in the country is made up of people whose ancestors were high-level government officials, successful businessmen, and educators, who were born in Seoul, attended the right high schools and universities (Kyung Ki High School and Seoul National University are the highest ranking schools in the country), live in a prestigious district of Seoul, and have a relative degree of family affluence.

Relationships and Connections

Among the hundreds of culturally loaded words that are windows to the etiquette and ethics of South Koreans, there are two that are especially meaningful in the business world: *yeon* (yohn) and *yonjul* (yohn-juhl). *Yeon* means "personal relationships," and *yonjul* means "personal connections."

In traditional Korean society all relations between and among people were based on and controlled by the existence, or non-existence, of a relationship—a blood tie, a school link, a work relationship, similar social class, or some prior involvement.

Virtually all life revolved around one or more of these relationships. One simply did not go out and establish a new relationship on the spot in order to make a new friend or accomplish a goal. Relationships that were unnecessary were virtually taboo. And generally speaking, social relationships and connections did not cross class lines.

When it became desirable or necessary to form a new relationship, the only approved way was through *yonjul*, that is, connections. To repeat the nation or state analogy, establishing new business relationships required going through a kind of diplomatic procedure that included introductions and a series of formal meetings.

South Korea still operates for the most part through connections. Businesspeople spend a lot of time and money creating and sustaining relationships with other individuals in companies and with government agencies.

Foreign companies in South Korea must go through the same process of developing and maintaining contacts, and some wisely identify and retain senior South Korean advisors or consultants who can quickly plug them into the kind of network that is essential for success in South Korea.

The dictates of *yeon* make it imperative that personal relations be established between two people before they can engage in business or interact socially. This personal relationship is established through acceptable introductions and then a number of face-to-face meetings that involve eating and drinking together, getting to know each other's personal background, and establishing common interests, trust, and confidence in each other.

Because the personal relationship must precede any business dealings, it requires an investment in time, effort, and money that the foreign businessperson is likely to regard as wasteful and foolish. And many foreigners, despite knowing about the requirements of *yeon*, will often ignore them and proceed as if they were in the U.S., where such personal requirements are minimal.

Yonjul, or "connections," are something South Koreans cannot do without. Virtually all areas of work and private life depend on making and maintaining networks of close personal connections.

The foreign businessperson who wants to succeed in South Korea must develop and nurture the same kind of networks.

The person in South Korea who seems to know everybody and is able to do almost anything through his connections is said to have a *bal i nulba* (bahl-ee-nool-bah), or "wide leg," instead of a "wide face" as in Japan. Because most business both within private industry and the government is based on having extensive personal contacts, the person with a "wide leg" is especially valued in South Korea.

Human Harmony in Management

The Korean-Confucian concept of harmony in human relations is expressed in the word *inhwa* (een-whah). It is a concept that incorporates both loyalty on the part of employees and maternal concern and behavior on the part of employers toward their workers.

LG (which was previously known as Lucky and Goldstar) was long regarded as the primary advocate of the *inhwa* style of management, and produced a book by that name that was used as a manual—some say "bible"—by the employees of the company. The guidelines in the manual include all of the traditional Confucian concepts of loyalty, unselfish goodwill, the maintenance of harmony in all human relations, respect for authority, plus a strong theme of South Korean spirit and South Korean nationalism based on some 5,000 years of historical accomplishments.

When LG established a factory in Huntsville, Alabama, the primary principles of *inhwa* were incorporated into its management philosophy, obviously with significant success.

Ties that Bind

Prior to the introduction of Western business practices in South Korea, virtually all business deals were made and kept on a foundation of trust and mutual obligation—a custom that worked well because in the absence of precise laws that was the only choice people had.

The whole framework of Korean society was, in fact, built on a foundation of *shinyong* (sheen-yohng), or trust, that was manifested through the etiquette and ethics of all relationships, beginning with the family unit and its members.

South Korean sociologists have even come up with a trust scale that shows how Koreans typically categorize people. Only members of the immediate family receive 100 percent on this trust scale. Nephews and nieces came in at 99 percent; cousins at 97 percent and other relatives at 96 percent. High school classmates were rated at 97 percent, and college classmates at 85 percent. People with the same family name, as well as those with ancestral homes in the same locale, came in at 70 percent.

Other Koreans with whom one had no relationship of any kind, and were strangers, came in as low as five percent. Foreigners with whom one had no relationship scored one percent.

Most present-day South Koreans say these assessments are much too narrow, but generally speaking, they continue to be applied in most life situations, including employment decisions. Until the early 1990s, most large South Korean corporations hired all of their employees from just one or two schools in order to take advantage of the built-in ties that existed among the graduates.

Given this mindset in the etiquette and ethics of South Korean businesspeople it is imperative for foreigners going into South Korea to be aware of the trust factor in their hiring and in developing a circle of business and government contacts in the country.

It is highly recommended that companies intending to do business in the country begin the process of establishing a network of contacts months, if not years, in advance. This can be done through embassies, chambers of commerce in South Korea, banks, service clubs (Rotarian and Kiwanis), professional associations, local groups of expatriate South Koreans, South Koreans attending schools in the country concerned, and the foreign subsidiaries of South Korean companies.

Generally speaking, it takes a minimum of three years before a newly arrived company and its managers are accepted into the South Korean business world, and only then if they are active outside of their offices and follow the rules of etiquette that are expected of all businesspeople.

The Importance of a Dignified Manner

The typical informal and often loud and rowdy behavior of many foreigners, which unfortunately often includes Americans, can be upsetting to Koreans whose traditional etiquette is highly refined and stylized.

Even the touching and backslapping behavior of ranking foreigners, done to express friendliness and goodwill, may be construed as undignified by more conservative South Koreans, who still live by a code of etiquette that was an integral part of their culture for some 2,000 years.

One of the main facets of this traditional code of etiquette was *wiom* (we-ohm), or dignity—a type of stylized behavior that included keeping emotions under control, maintaining an outward calm that concealed thoughts and protected "face," using the correct form of speech to whomever was being addressed, bowing and conforming to other types of body language dictated by the circumstances, and wearing the clothing appropriate for a person's class and position.

Still today most South Koreans conduct themselves with a degree of dignity that distinguishes them from other nationalities, and it is something that foreign businesspeople should be aware of and take into consideration when meeting and associating with their South Korean counterparts.

Wiom and "face" are closely associated in the South Korean mindset and they are especially sensitive to any remark or action that wounds their dignity (face), including such things as failure to use the title of a high-ranked individual, criticizing someone in public, or asking someone to do something that they do not feel is part of their duty, or is below them.

Traditionally, the only time South Koreans dispensed with their strict code of dignity was when they were drinking at an after-hours dinner party or gathering of some kind, and basically this still holds today among business associates. At such events, South Koreans expect any foreigners in the group to also drop their dignity shields and behave in an informal and sometimes rowdy and raunchy way—the latter if the gathering is in a cabaret or *kisaeng* house.

However, foreign businesspeople do not have to take a course in South Korean etiquette to get by without damaging someone's dignity. It is sufficient to be reserved and polite (by standards of Western etiquette), and let their South Korean counterparts set the tone.

Older South Koreans who are traditional in their attitudes and behavior put great stock in *wiom* and it is especially important for one to react properly toward them, meaning politely, with studied restraint and grace. This does not mean, of course, that one should compromise on ethics or principles in acknowledging this deeply entrenched social custom.

The Decision-Making System

The traditional South Korean system of decision-making is called *pummi* (poom-mee), or "proposal submitted for deliberation." But the system is more form than content, says Dr. Il Chung Whang, Dean of Business and Economics College, Han Yang University. Dr. Whang says the primary use of the *pummi* system is to diffuse responsibility, and that its use varies greatly with the size and type of company.

Proposals are written and then circulated vertically within the company. One of the most important functions of the *pummi* system, according to Dr. Whang, is to provide documentation for company programs.

However, the smaller the company, the less likely it is to depend on the consensus approach to decision-making. In fact, it is said that in all of South Korea, the only company that makes a concerted effort to follow the consensus approach to management is the Daewoo group, which fell on hard times. According to this view, the chief executive officer of each of the Daewoo companies expected all decisions to be unanimous, and he saw his role as asking questions and listening.

The process of decision-making in private industry in South Korea is similar to that in American companies that practice participation management. Senior managers have the authority to, and often do, make decisions on their own—especially in the case of founder-owners—but generally speaking, there is a considerable amount of consulting among middle and upper management before major decisions are made.

This process, which is quite different from the well-known Japanese system of "bottom-up" management by consensus, still requires a considerable degree of agreement among all levels of management, and therefore takes time to develop.

Foreigners approaching South Korean companies cannot confine their dealings to one or two individuals at the top. They must also develop cooperative relationships with all the section and department heads involved in their project.

Despite the surface similarities to Western management, the decision-making process within South Korean companies generally cannot be rushed—with the obvious exceptions being the "one-man" companies run by their founders or their equally strong-minded sons.

The area of decision-making in South Korea that stretches the typical Western businessman to the limits (and beyond) is government agencies and government-controlled organizations. Here, the situation is much more like it is in Japan, with a few added twists and turns that often amaze and frustrate foreigners who are not familiar with the psychology and processes that prevail in the ROK government.

Virtually every decision or action needed from the government or a government-controlled entity must be initiated at or near the lowest level of activity, and then work its way upward through the intricate, sensitive, vertically ranked departments. Because of the paranoia among government employees about being saddled with any kind of individual responsibility, and their obsession about covering every conceivable point (often from every conceivable angle), this process generally requires an inordinate amount of paperwork that would try the soul of any but a South Korean saint (and they couldn't possibly be immune to all suffering!).

Another aspect of interpersonal relations in the structure and psychology of South Korean society and business is that there is often very little communication and cooperation between vertically structured departments in a government agency or corporation. This frequently results in the outsider having to deal with different departments as if they were different agencies or companies.

Generally speaking, the Confucian values of South Korean society require that all decisions take into consideration the personal feelings and harmony of the group. The manager considering a proposition must give as much thought to its effects on the harmony of the group as to its business or economic benefits to the company. This need to maintain harmony is sometimes so overpowering that it takes precedence over strictly business considerations. When this happens to the unconditioned Western businessman, he may doubt both the goodwill and intelligence of the South Korean counterpart concerned.

This same cultural component of business in South Korea colors the entire management process, from the day-to-day flow of work to goal-setting and evaluation. It is an emotional, psychological aspect of business in South Korea that the Westerner must understand and deal with effectively to succeed.

In addition to contending with the need for group harmony, the Western businessman in South Korea must also be aware not to expect any significant degree of creativity from the average South Korean manager or worker. The harmony factor prevents a great deal of individual initiative that Westerners normally expect, but equally important in reducing creative thinking in South Korea is the rote system of learning used in schools. Not having been encouraged or allowed to think creatively, the average South Korean employee is more likely just to accept things as they are without question.

Western businessmen with extensive experience in South Korea add that South Korean workers often come up with shortcuts in how to do a particular job, but often without considering the consequences, so that the final results may be undesirable. In such situations, the Westerners add, the typical South Korean will say nothing about the problem and it will continue until noticed by someone else.

Tangchal yok (tahng chahl yahk), literally "power of insight," is the term used to describe the visceral feeling by which South Korean businessmen often make decisions—as opposed to using intellectual reasoning or logic. Because of the pervasive cultural conditioning Koreans undergo, they are also able to communicate to an extraordinary degree without using words, almost as if by telepathy.

Foreign businessmen dealing with South Koreans are often nonplussed by this system of decision-making and communicating and often waste a lot of time in trying to use logic when the South Korean side is seeking to develop personal rapport. Another interesting word that makes reference to the belly area is *baetchang* (bate-chahng), or "leather belly," which refers to a man who really has no assets but behaves as if he is rich.

Negotiating South Korean Style

The process of *kyosop* (k'yoh-sop), or negotiating, in South Korea is naturally a microcosm of the culture in action—a culture that remains very traditional in many ways. Koreans are tough and wily negotiators because their social experience is far more emotional and given to dramatic tactics than is common in the West. Their cultural conditioning means they express themselves in vague terms and keep their real intentions hidden until the last moment—which Westerners find irrational and upsetting.

Another Korean negotiating tactic is to swing back and forth between being confrontational and compromising—something that further upsets and imbalances Westerners, who are used to a straightforward, even keel approach in their negotiations. The Korean tactic is to wear the other side down and achieve their goals in small increments.

Westerners generally come to a negotiating table with their presentations in order and the perimeters of their authority firmly fixed. South Koreans generally come in without having settled all of the details of their position, and often have to stop the negotiations and consult with each other and others in the company.

(Notwithstanding this description, South Koreans point out strongly that they are generally more forthcoming and clearer than the Japanese in their negotiating style.)

Korean negotiators may switch their positions 180 degrees without any explanation for their actions—something Westerners also find unsettling. This, interestingly enough, is fairly common in all authoritarian, hierarchical societies. The rationale for this kind of behavior is that negotiators will maintain a certain position to the point where the threat of it backfiring appears imminent, and then reverse the stance as a protective measure.

This kind of behavior is difficult for Westerners to understand and accept because it often appears to be totally arbitrary and disruptive on purpose. It is arbitrary but it is also serious. The Korean negotiators are gambling that the other party will fold and they will win.

One of the explanations of this kind of behavior is the so-called "winner take all" attitude that is common in the Confucian sphere of Asia. Once failure becomes obvious and inevitable, the losing side subordinates itself to the winner without any psychic damage, and thereafter become enthusiastic collaborators and supporters—a common survival technique among people whose morality has traditionally been situational rather than based on fundamental principles.

Other aspects of the Korean negotiation style include throwing in some kind of surprise that catches the other side off guard, as in a chess game, and a degree of stubbornness that verges on being, or actually is, irrational. This surprise maneuver is known as *sunsu chida* (suun-suu chee-dah), which means "first to draw," or "first to strike."

Negotiation Dos and Don'ts

As already argued, Koreans are clever, forceful negotiators. They are not conditioned by any sense of fair play, of not taking advantage of a weaker adversary. They will take all they can get. In earlier times there was also the very strong feeling that foreigners had so much and they had so little that it was only right that they should get more than the foreign side did out of any deal.

One vital point the foreign businessman should keep in mind when negotiating any kind of arrangement in South Korea is to never let the Korean side know when you are scheduled to leave. If you do, they will invariably lead you on and wait until the last minutes or even seconds to inform you that they cannot accept your terms. This puts the foreigner under tremendous pressure to make last-minute concessions in order not to go home empty-handed. (The same caution applies to doing business in Japan.)

Typically, say old-timers, the visiting American businessman reacts in one of two ways: either he "gets hot, blows a gasket, and kills the deal, or he gives in and lets the South Koreans have what they want." A similar approach is often taken in labor-management negotiations, with union leaders assuming seemingly irreconcilable positions until the last few seconds of a deadline, when they will suddenly accept a compromise.

It is essential that the foreign negotiator know his own products and company, know clearly how flexible he can be, and be as knowledgeable as possible about his South Korean counterpart. Some foreign businessmen negotiate deals or make contracts with South Korean companies without leaving their hotels, having only a name and very general information about the South Korean side. Like their Japanese cousins, the South Koreans negotiate in groups and are masters at wearing opponents down. The more important the relationship, the more troops the foreign business-man should bring along.

One of the keys to successful negotiations in South Korea is to know in advance exactly who you will be facing, the number of people, their titles, specialties, and responsibilities. Matching them with a similar team of your own is a bare minimum. The best approach is to bring in people who are senior in age, experience, and authority.

When you are on South Korean turf, the managers of the meeting will direct you to the side of the table reserved for guests—the one facing the door. There is, of course, the usual small talk, with tea or some other soft drink served. Once the talks get underway, the South Korean side will generally be aggressive and sometimes loud. They can be blunt and apparently frank. These passionate outbursts should not be taken personally. It is part of the South Korean style.

You can demonstrate your own controlled passion, or let the South Korean side vent itself and then proceed in a calm, collected manner. Which method works best depends on the goals of the

South Korean party, how close or far apart the two sides are, and often the personality of the leading South Korean at the table.

The South Korean side will typically hold side discussions during the negotiating process, and will often not respond immediately to points or questions.

The Bargaining Factor in Business

Prior to the beginning of modern capitalism in Korea, which really did not take hold until well into the 20th century, prices for goods and services were generally arbitrary, depending on a variety of factors.

This situation, which existed from the beginning of Korean history, resulted in the people becoming skilled at *enuri* (eh-nuu-ree), or bargaining, and in bargaining becoming a national characteristic—something that people took for granted and did automatically. Most prices are set in South Korea's brick-and-mortar places today, but in street stalls and markets *enuri* is still the order of the day and being good at bargaining is regarded as a necessary social skill.

Few contemporary Westerners have had more than "tourist experiences" of bargaining, are usually not good at it, are reluctant to do it, and generally get taken advantage of when they try.

Westerners who get into bargaining situations in South Korea are also at a furthur disadvantage because the Korean approach to the process is emotional. If they encounter any kind of real resistance on the part of a potential buyer, they tend to become loud and passionate.

In Korea, these displays of passion are recognized and understood "acts" that are part of the process, and thoroughly enjoyed by the players. These sessions are described as *chugoni-batkoni* (chuu-goh-nee bath-koh-nee), or "give-and-take," as well as *oksinkaksin* (ohk-sheenpkahk-sheen), or "pushing back and forth."

Not surprisingly, South Korean businesspeople bring their bargaining skills and techniques to the negotiating table when dealing with Westerners, who have generally been conditioned to use facts and logic to argue their cases.

Foreign businesspeople should be forewarned that there will

likely be a great deal of emotionally charged stagecraft in their negotiations with South Koreans, and be prepared to calmly ride them out—or if they are secure in their position, throw a few emotional punches of their own.

Controlling Competition

Part of the etiquette and ethics of traditional South Korea was the cultural and political imperative that *kyongjaeng* (k'yohng-jang), or competition, be categorized and controlled by the government and by custom to avoid friction and maintain social harmony. This, in part, was in keeping with the Buddhist concept that competition that resulted in some people being better off than others was immoral.

This system was another of the many factors that worked to repress innovation and invention during Korea's long feudal period. This system, however, primarily applied to individuals acting on their own. Competition between families, communities, and commercial enterprises was not considered immoral as long as it was done on a group basis. And within families and other groups, individuals could and did compete fiercely.

With the end of the feudal laws dictating Korean behavior in the middle of the 20th century, Koreans took to individual competition with a focus and energy that is remarkable. South Koreans today do not like to lose or come second in any endeavor, whether it is sports, working, entertaining, or doing whatever.

Individual South Koreans see themselves as representing their immediate family, their relatives, their community, and the whole nation. They are driven by a compulsion to excel and succeed.

This cultural characteristic is another of the factors that played a role in the rise of South Korea to economic prominence, and continues to make South Koreans among the most competitive of all workers.

Hospitality and Business

One of the most interesting—and often startling—aspects of Korea's traditional etiquette and ethics is the role of *hwandae* (hwahn-die), or hospitality. Koreans are among the most hospitable people on the planet, and in business situations their hospitality can be so aggressive that it surprises and sometimes shocks Western visitors.

Like most Asians and some Westerners, Koreans have traditionally marked special occasions with sumptuous meals and the uninhibited consumption of alcoholic drinks. In business situations in earlier times it was customary for Koreans to lay on the *hwandae*, frequently to the point that they literally forced guests to drink.

A lady of my personal acquaintance, the CEO of a medium-sized high-tech company, recently went to Seoul to meet her South Korean agent. After meetings all day, the president of the agency insisted on taking her out for a barbecue beef dinner and drinks. Within a short time, he was drunk and became even more aggressive in trying to get her to drink, and in comments about his marriage and sex affairs when he was away from home.

The lady was embarrassed, and as the evening wore on, became more and more angry. The two young male aides to the president who accompanied them were obviously aware that their boss was going too far but they said and did nothing. At about 2 a.m. in the morning the lady escaped by literally crawling under the low South Korean-style floor table and running out of the restaurant.

This incident was no doubt more shocking to a lady than it would have been to a man, but it was not unusual behavior for a South Korean businessman during those days.

Foreign businesspeople who do not want to over-drink or abuse themselves by staying out late beyond a reasonable hour, should not hesitate to make a plausible-sounding excuse or explanation to limit their drinking and end the evening at a decent hour. This is one of a growing number of occasions when not doing things the South Korean way is right.

Foreign visitors should also keep in mind the Western custom of "going Dutch," or sharing costs, is alien to the traditional Korean way of thinking and behaving, especially where businesspeople are concerned. The exceptions are students and close friends who frequently go out or stop in some place for drinks and are not trying to impress anybody.

In the case of South Korean businesspeople, politicians and the like, they gain face by acting as the host, and the more elaborate the dinner or party, the more face they gain. This often puts Western businesspeople who are on tight company budgets in a bind because they cannot match the freewheeling ways of their South Korean counterparts.

Private Invitations

South Koreans are enthusiastic hosts and tend to be much more open in their relationships with foreigners than most other Asians, particularly older-generation Japanese.

In Japan, people traditionally did not entertain friends in their homes—in part because their homes were small and crowded. The custom was—and generally still is—to treat friends and visitors at restaurants, bars, and nightclubs.

South Koreans on the other hand, particularly those in the middle and upper classes, delight in inviting foreign guests to their homes for meals that are more like banquets than daily fare. Those who have traveled abroad or are engaged in international business take special pleasure in extending *chodai* (choh-die) or "invitations" to foreign guests.

The openness demonstrated through the custom of inviting foreign guests into their homes is one of the reasons why many foreigners find working and living in South Korea more natural and more satisfying than what is generally experienced in some other Asian countries.

Business Dining

When invitations for a meal are extended to you they should be accepted as well as reciprocated within a reasonable amount of time during your visit. Dinner is the largest meal of the day, and usually takes place between 6:00 p.m. and 8:00 p.m.

Entertaining frequently takes place in restaurants and coffee shops. If you are invited to someone's home, consider it an honor and think carefully if you intend to refuse.

The person who extends an invitation for breakfast, lunch, or dinner is expected to pay for the meal. If you want to pay for a dinner party a common tactic is to pretend to go to the washroom a little before the party ends, and pick up the bill from the cashier or server and pay before anyone else can.

In dining, the traditional protocol is to wait for the eldest person or honored guest to start eating first. It is a polite gesture to follow this custom.

Tipping is still not common in South Korean restaurants. A service charge of 15 percent or more is automatically included in restaurant and hotel bills. However, some diners leave a tip if the service is exceptional.

Business Drinking

As in many societies, drinking alcoholic beverages in South Korea was originally linked with religious rituals, apparently because it was believed that it was possible to commune more directly with the gods when in a drunken or trance-like state.

In earlier times Korean women were allowed to drink, but with the introduction of a more strict form of Confucianism in 1392, the role of women in society changed dramatically, and drinking was one of the many things that became taboo for the female population.

Men drank at religious rituals, during festivals, and at "after hours" dinners or parties with male friends. Drinking became especially important to men in this highly structured and layered society, because that was the only time they could dispense with Korea's restrictive interpersonal protocol that controlled their behavior at other times.

When industrialization came to Korea in the 20th century, *kyojesul* (k'yoh-jeh-suul), or "business drinking," became an integral part of developing and maintaining interpersonal relationships between coworkers, suppliers, and customers.

Still today, *kyojesul* plays a key role in formal company affairs, such as celebrations to mark the end of successful meetings with outside contacts, entertaining guests, customers, and government officials, in after-hours coworker sessions that are designed to build company loyalty and spirit, and to air grievances that cannot be addressed during working hours because of the culture of saving face and a powerful need to avoid hurting anyone's feelings.

Foreigners who are new to South Korea may be put off by the change in Korean behavior at drinking sessions. They typically become much more aggressive in their demeanor, invariably insisting that their guests drink heartily—often to excess—and may not take "no" for an answer.

There is a ritualized etiquette in such after-hours drinking. Members of the host party, beginning with the chief host, insist on repeatedly pouring drinks for guests, even when their glasses are not empty.

Leaving your glass full to limit the volume you drink doesn't work. Host members will insist that you take a drink to partially empty your glass every time they approach you—which can be every minute or so during an evening.

Aggressiveness during drinking parties is part of the effusiveness of South Korean hospitality, but it also derives from a desire to get a guest drunk to see how he or she behaves when the strict daytime rules of etiquette go by the wayside.

Most South Korean businessmen have *sulchinku* (suhl-cheen-kuu), or "drinking partners," whom they meet regularly to relieve stress by getting things off their chest, and to network and get help when they need it.

This is a custom that is highly recommended for foreign businesspeople who are stationed in South Korea or visit the country regularly, since *sulchinku* can be invaluable sources of cultural advice and connections.

In any event, "business drinking" continues to play a key role in the etiquette and ethics of South Korean businesspeople and government officials. It is an important part of the culture, and should not but ignored by foreign businesspersons.

Tangol (tahn-gole), literally a "sweet place," is a bar where a businessman has developed a close relationship with the owner or manager and the hostesses, and is treated as a special customer. It is a place he takes new friends and clients, and where he goes when he needs to have attractive women fuss over him and make him feel good. Such bars are also called *tanga* (tahn-gah).

The practice of keeping one's own bottle at a favorite bar, called *Bottle-Keep* (boe-tahl-kee-puu), has been introduced into South Korea from Japan, but it is not as widespread. "We drink so much there is almost never anything left in a bottle to leave at a bar," said a South Korean executive, laughing.

Bangsuk ul galda (bahng-suuk ule gall-dah) literally means "to put a cushion under someone" (to make sitting more comfortable). It is used in reference to wining, dining, and otherwise catering to a person you want something from—for which South Koreans have a special talent.

Still today, most South Korean men who do not have health problems drink, and refusing to drink with them without an acceptable excuse is regarded as unfriendly if not anti-social. However, some younger South Koreans now resist the pressure to drink heavily and abstinence or moderate drinking is more acceptable.

Acceptable excuses for not drinking at all include a health problem and religious beliefs. However, if you do not drink, it can become awkward for you and for your South Korean hosts or guests, since they will drink and have a raucous and often rowdy time while you remain sober.

At business parties it is common for members of the hosting group to make the rounds, refilling the glasses of seniors and guests. In some cases the senior South Korean host will begin this process by refilling the glass of the guests in the order of their rank. The larger the group, the more people may join in the rounds, and the more pressure there is to drink to excess.

One approach, even if you are a non-drinker, is to take tiny sips of beer or some other relatively weak drink and then simulate the level of tipsy behavior that keeps you in tune with the group. (I have also surreptitiously dumped drinks in flowerpots.) Whatever the situation, when you do not want your glass refilled, empty it, then turn it upside down on the table.

When your glass is being refilled it is polite to hold it with one hand, supporting that hand with the other hand.

Another custom where individuals in a group want to demonstrate the closeness of their relationship is for two individuals to exchange drinking glasses or cups and toast each other.

When the party is in a hostess club or a karaoke bar, it almost always includes singing after everyone has loosened up. Guests are expected to sing. If you are not up to singing solo, dragging a cohort or a member of the South Korean group onto the stage to sing with you is acceptable.

Singing Your Way to Success

It might sound far-fetched to Western businesspeople who have not been to South Korea (or Japan) to suggest that they should brush up on their singing as part of their preparations for any trip to the country.

In fact, singing either in groups or solo performances before live audiences has been a part of the cultural tradition of Koreans since ancient times. *Norae* (noh-rye), or singing, began as part of shamanistic rituals and celebrations that required the participation of everyone.

From this very early tradition, singing became a form of folk entertainment and played an even more important role in the lives of people. Chinese travelers on the Korean peninsula in 1000 B.C. reported that in a number of the tribal nations they visited it was customary for the people to gather around open campfires in the evening and hold impromptu songfests. The Chinese visitors wrote that in one tribe the people devoted the entire month of October to singing and dancing.

The royal courts that later developed in Korea maintained troupes of professional singers and dancers to entertain the royal families, ministers, and state visitors. One of the primary skills of Korea's professional warrior class, which first appeared during the Silla dynasty (57 B.C. to A.D. 669), was singing and dancing.

As time passed, all Koreans began singing for the pleasure of it, and over the millennia learning a large number of folk songs in early childhood became an integral part of childhood. Thereafter, people sang throughout their lives, at parties, at festivals and other types of celebrations.

The most famous of Korea's professional singers were the *kisaeng* (kee-sang), young women chose for their beauty and taught from an early age to sing, dance, play musical instruments, and provide titillating company to men (preceding Japan's more famous *geisha* by more than 1,000 years). In the 1890s, before the last Korean dynasty ended in 1910, there were some 10,000 *kisaeng* attached to the royal court in Seoul.

Suffice to say that singing has had a long and important role in Korean history, and continues to be an important feature of modern Korean society. Many Koreans follow the tradition of engaging in *jang ki* (jahng kee), which means "favorite technique," and refers to privately practicing some skill—usually singing—so that when they perform in public they will not embarrass themselves and will impress people.

South Korea also imported the *karaoke* (kah-rah-oh-kay) boom that started in Japan, and went one better with a proliferation of *norae bang* (noh-rye bahng), or "singing salons," that went well beyond the karaoke bars in Japan.

Businesspeople sing at dinner and drinking parties—both of which are an integral part of doing business in South Korea—as well as at celebrations and other events.

Any foreign businessperson who spends three or more nights in South Korea is almost invariably invited to an evening out where singing is part of the action—and may be expected to sing.

In earlier times, Koreans naturally assumed that everyone could sing, but where most Europeans, and especially Americans, were concerned, they soon learned better. But that hasn't dampened Koreans' enthusiasm—they still insist that everyone sing, and this insistence can be quite aggressive.

The foreign businessman who really wants to do well in South Korea will need to learn how to sing. That is a very big order for most Westerners, but it can be one of the most valuable skills to develop. Singing is an important part of the upbringing of Koreans, and is institutionalized at eating and drinking parties, where businessmen unwind, relax, enjoy themselves, and do the psychic communication that is so important to the well-being of their emotions, spirit, and mood—and image of other people.

Foreign businessmen are expected to participate in these nighttime singing sessions, and not being able or willing to join in, no matter how badly one might perform, is a serious handicap. As silly as it might seem, any foreign businessman expecting to go to South Korea should first lock himself in his bathroom (or go out into the desert, open fields, or mountains) and practice belting out two or three oldies that he is probably at least vaguely familiar with. Being a really good singer is seen as a talent that is just as valuable as other desirable life skills—and sometimes more so, because in Korea, it contributes directly to close communication and feelings of friendship and well-being.

In any event, it is the effort that matters, not the quality of the singing.

Having Fun in a *Kisaeng* House

Japan's *geisha* and the term "geisha house" are well known around the world, but what is not so well known is that Korea had *kisaeng* (the Korean equivalent of *geisha*), hundreds of years before the appearance of the first *geisha* in Japan.

Korea's *kisaeng* date from the period of the Three Kingdoms, roughly 57 B.C. to A.D. 669. Rather than having first been associated with prostitution, as in Japan, the *kisaeng* were young, upper-class girls trained in singing, dancing, and pleasuring men who were attached to the royal court for the convenience of the king, senior ministers, and important visitors.

At first called *yorak* (yoh-rahk), or "entertainers," the number of these young women increased over the generations, and because they intermingled with men on the highest level in the country they were often primary actors in illicit romances and scandals.

In the late 15th and early 16th centuries, the newly-crowned king of the Choson dynasty increased the number of *kisaeng* attached to the court from 100 to 10,000 (and referred to his chief *kisaeng* recruiter as his "red skirt envoy").

The royal recruiters scoured the country, looking for the prettiest girls—and once selected, they were the only females in the country who were permitted to become educated. Their training included reading, writing, composing poetry, playing musical instruments, singing, and dancing. They were also instructed in a variety of topics designed to make them interesting conversationalists for men—something Korean wives did not do with their husbands.

Following this extraordinary move by the Choson king, the recruiting, training, feeding, dressing, and managing the *kisaeng* became a major commercial enterprise with hundreds of support personnel. They were the only women in Korea who could wear makeup and gorgeous clothing, and did not have to avert their eyes when passing males. They could also smile and talk as much as they pleased—something that was denied to other women.

Another rule established by the Choson king was that all *kisaeng* had to retire at the age of 30, so they could be replaced by younger girls who had been recruited when they were eight or nine years old, and trained until they were 15 and had become full-fledged *kisaeng*.

Although *kisaeng* were officially prohibited from marrying, the majority became mistresses and some became second wives. Many became nationally famous for their beauty and artistic accomplishments, and some became wealthy as a result of gifts from rich patrons.

There were several categories and ranks of *kisaeng* during the last centuries of the Choson era, including one category that was trained as doctors to administer to women, since male doctors were not permitted to touch female patients.

During the 19th century, the thousands of *kisaeng* attached to the royal court were made available to all upper class men who could afford their fees. The men in many wealthy families bankrupted themselves in their pursuit of the pleasure girls.

The *kisaeng* formed a union between 1897 and 1906. Separated from the royal court in 1910 with the end of the Choson dynasty, they came under the control of private managers.

Today, every city of any size has its *kisaeng* houses, and while they include some of the most beautiful women in the world, their skills are generally limited to dancing, singing, talking, and making men feel good. Some of the *kisaeng* (and nightclub hostesses) are, in fact, so gorgeous that Western patrons are likely to drool at the sight of them.

Taking guests to *kisaeng* houses is an integral part of the South

Korean way of establishing and sustaining business relation-ships. Most foreign businessmen who go to South Korea and have Korean contacts are taken to *kisaeng* houses for dinner and entertainment.

The Job Rotation System

Larger South Korean corporations typically rotate their younger white-collar employees between departments and branches in the early spring as part of their on-the-job training. This system is referred to as *insa idong* (een-sah ee-dong), or "job rotation."

The purpose of this system is, of course, to familiarize new managerial and executive candidates with all of the key depart-ments and divisions of the company, and to ensure that they become acquainted with others to facilitate communication in the years ahead.

There are obviously many benefits to the *insa idong* system, but it has a downside as well, not only for the Korean company, but also for foreigner businesspeople who deal with the com-pany. Because key sections in the company have a regular stream of new recruits who are inexperienced, the overall productivity of the sections is lower than it would be if staffed only by expe-rienced veterans.

Since the purpose of rotating young employees into new jobs is to give them experience, they are assigned tasks they have never done before and must go through a steep learning curve. One of the tasks that is typically assigned to newcomers is interfacing with foreign visitors and customers.

It therefore often happens that managing the product or service of a foreign company is left in the hands of young people with lim-ited experience. It takes anywhere from one or two years to three or four years for a foreign company to develop a good, efficient, productive relationship with a South Korean agent or joint ven-ture partner—a process that can be adversely affected by having to deal with a new contact every year or so.

About the only practical way to counter what can be a serious handicap caused by the *insa idong* system is to keep the section or department chiefs and their deputies in the communications loop so they will be informed of what is, or is not, going on.

However, if foreign companies can hang in and succeed in South Korea despite the job rotating system, it can gradually lead to significant success in their overall relationships, because they will end up knowing managers in many parts of the South Korean company.

Company Mottos and Creeds

Any understanding and appreciation of South Korean etiquette and ethics in business must include the values and expectations implicit in the word *sahun* (sah-hoon), which translates broadly as "company instructions," but in reality is more of a statement or motto that encapsulates a company's corporate philosophy and aspirations.

Both the philosophy and the goals of the typical South Korean company, as expressed in its *sahun*, are invariably based on the highest ethical and moral standards, on insuring the survival and growth of the company, and making a contribution to society in general as well as to the nation.

In other words, *sahun* are designed to have the practical, nationalistic, and spiritual content that the South Korean psyche demands. Among the elements typically found in company mottos are expressions that come under the term *chango* (chahng-goh), which refers to creativity and entrepreneurial spirit.

In addition to *sahun*, South Korean companies have *jimmu kyuchik* (jeem-muu k'yuu-cheek), or "company rules," and a reading of the rules of a particular company reveals a great deal about the etiquette and ethics that are aimed at shaping and controlling the conduct of employees.

Foreign companies setting up operations in South Korea are well advised to come up with *sahun* of their own that fit the sentiments and aspirations of their employees, along with company rules that spell out, in the most precise terms, the conditions of employment down to the last dot.

Dealing with Office Stress

Pulda (puhl-dah) is the Korean term for "office stress"—that is, the stress that builds up in Korean companies because of having to conform to precise rules of etiquette and to work at an inhumanly fast pace in a highly competitive atmosphere.

Foreign managers in South Korea seldom if ever attempt to use full-fledged Korean management techniques, but there is invariably some degree of *pulda* buildup in any group of Koreans because of the requirements of their etiquette and because they set such high standards for themselves.

Both South Korean and foreign firms deal with the *pulda* factor by sponsoring periodic events that are designed to relieve stress. These include sporting events and eating and drinking parties at which both inferiors and superiors can behave more or less as equals, temporarily dispensing with the strict protocol that controls their relationship at other times.

These *pulda*-relieving events sometimes include humorous skits in which the roles of inferiors and superiors are switched, with lower ranking employees getting to order their bosses around—a cultural tradition that is ancient in Korea.

In fact, during Korea's long feudal age the only way common people could criticize superiors, the social system, and the government was in humorous plays that were presented as entertainment. Now that the feudal system is no longer the law of the land, and the calm that was long associated with Korea is no longer enforced with a heavy hand, most urban South Koreans live in the fast lane, with all of the tension that one can experience driving down a crowded freeway at well above the speed limit.

The pace of business in South Korea is such that many Western residents and visiting businesspeople can't wait to get back to New York or some other such place where life is easier.

Advice for Foreign Managers

Harmonious labor-management relations in South Korea require a much larger personal commitment of time and resources than is typical in the average Western company. International business consultant Song-Hyon Jang, president of S. H. Jang and Associates

Inc., lists some of the keys to achieving the necessary harmony as: multilevel communications, a competitive compensation package, interpersonal company activities, scrupulously fair treatment, and a documented work policy.

"It is particularly important for expatriate managers to open natural but discreet communications channels with their Korean staff, on different levels in all departments," notes Jang. "A deliberate avoidance of bureaucratic protocol will make the head office more accessible to the employees, allowing lines of communication to develop. As long as there is a conscious effort to remove all obstacles and restrictions to a free flow of communication between labor and management, disputes can be prevented or defused. However, in communication with labor, management has to preserve a benevolent but firm and consistent position. Koreans have learned how to respect authority," he adds.

Avoiding Cultural Backlash

The Western concept of democracy has taken firm root in South Korea but there are cultural limits to individualism, especially in large corporations that are generally managed more or less like fiefdoms—a system that is directly responsible for the production and competitive power of South Korean companies.

South Koreans appreciate the concept of *tongnip* (tohn-neep), or "personal independence," in principle, and they apply it to their lives in areas that do not directly impact on others. But generally speaking, Korean companies still function according to the ancient Confucian notion of groupism. Individualistic behavior within a group situation generally creates friction and ill-will—unless the individual concerned is the founder/owner.

Still today, some South Koreans, particularly those who are more traditional in their mindset and behavior, look upon Western-style individualism and independence as selfish, since it often gives precedence to the individual at the expense of others.

It pays for the foreigner doing business in South Korea to be sensitive to any possible backlash resulting from their own individualistic behavior, or expecting or demanding individualistic behavior from their South Korean contacts or employees.

The Role of "Go-Betweens"

Unlike in the United States and other Western countries, in Korea disputes were traditionally handled by *chungjaein* (chuung-jay-een), or private mediators, rather than using a legal system of lawyers, judges, and courts.

In feudal Korea (prior to 1910), the legal system consisted of a relatively small number of edicts published by the various courts over hundreds of years—most of which were based on Confucian principles—and government officials who had acted as judge and jury on their own.

The Confucian-oriented court did not believe in establishing comprehensive laws to govern the populace, preferring instead to give authorities at various levels leeway to make their own rulings and to interpret existing laws according to the circumstances.

Because decisions made by incumbent authorities were therefore arbitrary, and were generally not based on universal concepts of justice or fairness, people with disputes avoided going to the authorities with their problems, preferring instead to use *chungjaein*.

Since the downfall of the Choson dynasty in 1910, and especially since the implementation of a democratic form of government in South Korea from around 1960 onwards, Koreans have established a legal system that is patterned more or less after the Western model.

Today, however, there are fundamental differences in South Korea's approach to the law and the settling of disputes. Until the 1990s, lawyers did not "work for" their clients. They worked for the courts, and their primary purpose was to represent the government and the government's interpretation of laws.

This situation has changed dramatically, and there are now lawyers who represent clients in the Western sense. But generally speaking, South Koreans still prefer to use *chungjaein* to settle disputes, because it goes against their cultural grain to get in conflict with government authorities on any level and in any way.

Western businesspeople are well advised to first take the mediator route to settling any legal-type problems they have in South Korea. Going to the courts should only be pursued as a last resort—

keeping in mind that the level of "justice" in South Korea contin-ues to vary depending on the issue, the parties in a dispute, and the region of the country where the dispute occurs.

Just as foreign companies operating in South Korea should have a good Korean consultant on staff, or readily available, it also makes good sense to have access to people who have a good track record as professional mediators.

The Need for Patience

When the foreigner first arrives in South Korea, whether to engage in business or diplomacy, one of the many things he or she is told is that the most important attribute they must have is *chamulsong* (chah-muhl-song), or "patience"—that without almost infinite patience their progress will be difficult and much less likely to lead to success.

While Korean philosophers have long looked upon *chamulsong* as being one of their country's most admirable traits, they did not bother to consider that Koreans appeared to be patient because they had absolutely no viable choice.

Historically, any attempt to speed things beyond what was morally and culturally acceptable was so un-Korean that it could be life threatening. Change was seen as not only anti-Confucian, but politically forbidden because the reigning powers liked things the way they were.

Patience is still a very important asset when doing business in South Korea, partly because of continuing cultural restraints on taking fast actions before a solid consensus is reached, but also because the government agencies involved in guiding and control-ling business activities tend to be bureaucratic.

Furthermore, government bureaucrats in South Korea do not necessarily follow the letter of the law in approving things. There is typically a personal and an emotional element in their behavior that can add days, weeks, or months to their actions—and often require that considerable outside pressure and/or some other step be taken by the petitioner before a matter is settled.

On an individual basis, South Koreans can be as impatient and as outspoken as anyone else, but when it involves a company or a government agency they generally cannot act on their own and must be very circumspect in dealing with others so as not to make things worse.

Naturally, the larger the number of people involved in any situation, the longer it generally takes to achieve a consensus and get a result. Overt efforts to speed things up in a non-Korean way are more likely to slow them down.

Formula for Keeping Best Workers

Consultant S. H. Jang says that for the foreign company in South Korea to achieve sustained growth and success, it is imperative that it have a competitive compensation scheme, otherwise the company will continuously lose its best workers to other firms with better pay packages. When companies are too small to be competitive in direct compensation, or have budgetary restraints for any reason, Jang recommends such benefits as stock offers, pension plans, unemployment insurance, and health care plans.

Developing Team Spirit

One of the most effective ways to build team spirit and a family-like atmosphere in the foreign company in South Korea is to sponsor such activities as picnics, sports activities, a company newsletter or newspaper, and recreational clubs.

Perhaps the most important aspect of managing a South Korean work force, however, is to be scrupulously fair to all employees and avoid favoring any particular employee for any reason. "It is sometimes necessary to go beyond the stipulations of labor law," says consultant Jang, "especially in a case where family members of top executives are involved in the business organization."

Jang adds: "Without compromising standards, the manager's handling of mistakes made by staff members requires a great deal of diplomacy and understanding to prevent them from losing face. To avoid office tensions and belligerence, fair, just treatment by the manager is crucial. Proper treatment will tend to weld the loyalty of office personnel to the manager and raise the degree of efficiency and quality of their work." Jang goes on to say that it is essential for foreign employers to have their employment regulations, office procedures, and work rules in writing and have them signed by all new employees.

"Once a complaint is filed by an employee against company executives, labor authorities tend to support the employee, so a signed agreement can save a lot of trouble," Jang added.

The Use of Collective Punishment

One of the primary foundations of traditional Confucian societies (and Korea was long been described as the most Confucian of all Asian nations) was collective responsibility and *chebol* (cheh-bohl), or collective punishment.

In early Korea *chebol* was practiced with religious zeal as one of the main measures of maintaining absolute stability. Whole families, even whole villages, were held responsible for the behavior of each member, creating an inhuman system that turned people into virtual robots obsessed with following prescribed rules and customs. *Chebol* is not a part of modern-day South Korea's legal system, but the concept remains a part of the psyche of older Koreans, resulting in them being especially watchful and concerned about the behavior of family members.

South Koreans are especially sensitive about being subjected to collective punishment of any kind, particularly by foreign countries and foreign companies. Foreign business managers in South Korea should therefore be especially careful to individualize any sanctions they might impose on employees.

Veterans' Law

Because of its system of mandatory military service for all males, the ROK has a Veterans' Administration Law that requires all firms in South Korea with 20 or more employees to hire veterans, their spouses, and their children in proportion to the overall number of employees. All foreign companies setting up operations in South Korea are subject to this law and must take it into consideration in their hiring practices.

When employers are unable to find their minimum quota of veterans and their family members, the government provides them.

Foreign Workers

South Korean companies have few racial or cultural qualms about employing Western workers in their domestic offices and factories. Major employers of foreign talent include the country's top conglomerates, such as Hyundai, Samsung, and LG. Among the hundreds of such employees are engineers, scholars, consultants, and attorneys.

Emphasis on Company Training

Larger South Korean companies have rigorous procedures for selecting new employees, with each company striving to get the best and brightest of the annual crop of university graduates. The process begins with stiff screening examinations in which the competition may be as high as 100:1. Once accepted into a company, an equally rigorous training program begins, lasting from two to five months, and incorporating both "brainwashing" and "survival techniques." The purpose of the training programs goes beyond just giving the new employee the necessary knowledge and skills to make a contribution to the company's efforts. They are aimed at molding the newcomers to fit the company's organizational pattern and culture.

The training tends to emphasize attitude instead of professional skills, the idea being that dedication, loyalty, and team spirit take precedence over initial competence.

These company training programs include intensive courses in foreign languages, particularly English, with the trainees sometimes being sent to university-level language institutes. The companies thus make a longterm investment in their most promising managerial candidates.

Samsung Electronics Co., Ltd., founded in 1938 and generally listed as the oldest company in South Korea's business history, is famous—or notorious, depending on the source—for its managerial system and its personnel training program, which has been described as "incredibly inhuman." Because of its emphasis on tough training for its employees, the company is frequently referred to as the "Samsung Academy," and is regarded as a good training center for South Korean businessmen.

Samsung's founder, Lee Byung-chul, carried "report cards" on every executive in the company, and used the cards at the beginning of each year to decide who was to be promoted or demoted.

Arbitration Taboos

As is typical in Confucian-oriented societies, South Koreans abhor the idea of outsiders becoming involved in their business affairs, which they regard as personal. Until recent times, Western-style arbitration was not regarded as a logical or viable choice. When South Koreans were forced to accept arbitration, the decisions were invariably Korean-style compromises—the kind of solutions they preferred to work out on their own.

Times have changed. There is now a Korean Arbitration Board (KAB) that is very active, and is generally held in high regard by the foreign business community. English language translations are provided, and in some cases the proceedings are conducted in English. But arbitration through the KAB may be lengthy and expensive.

AmCham continues to advise foreign companies in an attempt to get American or ICC arbitration rules from Geneva written into any joint-venture agreement, while noting, however, that the South Korean side may strongly oppose the move.

The moral, of course, is to try to avoid the official arbitration process in South Korea.

South Koreans hate the idea of *chungjae*, or "arbitration by outsiders," and go to extreme lengths to avoid it. They regard such a move by company executives as a public admission of their incompetency and general unfitness to direct a company's affairs. Private "mediation" between the parties involved is the accepted method of resolving disputes. The experienced mediator (*chung-jaein*) is therefore an important person in South Korean society. The same word also means "middleman" and "intermediary."

The Importance of the Apology

In Confucian-oriented societies, the apology has traditionally played a similar role to that of confessions in the Catholic religion, where you confess your sins, God forgives you, and you start over with a clean slate.

The traditional etiquette in Korea, which covered all personal as well as official relationships, was so detailed, so strict, and so limiting that mistakes and general failures to live up to all of the requirements were so common that apologizing, often even before a social indiscretion had occurred, became an institutionalized and virtually ritualized custom.

When individuals committed relatively minor infractions of the law or any other accepted custom that resulted in the authorities becoming involved, a teary *sagwa* (sahg-wah), or apology, was often enough to get the offender off with no more than a reprimand. If the offense was serious, an apology mitigated the level of punishment. If a person refused to apologize—guilty or not—the punishment was invariably much more harsh.

The *sagwa* continues to play an important role in South Korean society in personal as well as business and professional relationships. Some offenses require only a verbal apology. Others require a *simal so* (she-mahl soh), or "letter of apology."

Foreigners in South Korea, businesspeople as well as others, should be aware of the importance of the apology in the etiquette and ethics of South Koreans, and make appropriate use of it.

Because of the strict system of etiquette, South Koreans find that frequent apologies on all kinds of occasions, including what may appear to be trifling concerns to outsiders, are the better part of valor.

The Korean Adaptation of English

South Korea, like Japan, has adopted thousands of English words and made them a key part of the South Korean vocabulary. Unlike the Japanese, however, South Koreans do not feel compelled to Koreanize everything that comes into the country.

In Japan, foreign words are Japanized and pronounced as if they were Japanese—with the result that it is often extremely difficult, and sometimes impossible, for foreign students of Japanese to divine the meaning of the formerly English terms. For example, *sabaiburu* (sah-by-buu-ruu) is "survival" pronounced in Japanese. Unless read or heard in a very clear and specific context, *sabaiburu* is meaningless to the native English speaker.

Rather than go this route, in 1985 the South Korean Ministry of Education adopted a system of writing foreign words using the Korean alphabet, which maintains, as far as possible, the original pronunciation. This farsighted move has made a significant contribution to the ability of South Koreans and English-speaking people to communicate with each other.

Dos and Don'ts

Every foreign businessman who has spent any significant length of time in South Korea has his own list of "dos and don'ts" for conducting business in the ROK. Virtually all of these lists begin with the need to establish a network of strong personal friendships inside and outside of the government, nurturing them carefully and continuously.

Almost all actions one takes, personal and business, are fundamentally influenced by one's network of friends. The government plays such an important role in business in South Korea that it is essential to identify the appropriate ministries, agencies, offices, and officials as early as possible and immediately begin the process of developing and massaging that network.

Your commitment to South Korea should be longterm, and the man who comes in and sets up the operation should be prepared to remain in South Korea for several years—certainly a minimum of three—and this is cutting it very thin. When transfers are made, it is vital that the replacement be brought in early—like a year or more in advance—to give him time to take over the established network of friends and contacts.

And again, this is not something that can be handled "American style," just by taking the newcomer around, introducing him, and then leaving him on his own. The depth and quality of personal relationships necessary to function effectively comes only with time. Patience, good emotional control, a sense of humor, and a longterm perspective are keys for doing well in South Korea.

Despite appearances, it is generally unwise to leave important decisions—or in many cases, routine decisions—to the South Korean side, even when you are dealing with a very internationalized individual with extensive experience, unless you are willing to accept the consequences of decisions reflecting a strong South Korean flavor. Along the same lines, the foreign businessman in South Korea cannot leave marketing arrangements up to personal connections, although personal relationships may play a key role in setting up a marketing program.

Other hard-knocks wisdom suggested by veteran businessmen on the scene include:

- don't leave government approval up to a South Korean partner;
- don't locate a joint-venture firm in the same building as your South Korean partner;
- make sure you control (with experienced advice) all hiring and placement.

Regulation by Competitors

As extraordinary as it might seem, there are several industries in which South Korean companies in effect regulate the activities of their foreign competitors. These industries include advertising, banking, insurance, transportation, trading, engineering, and construction.

Generally, this regulation is effected through industry associations that foreign firms cannot join, or if they can join they are limited to a type of membership that has no power or influence. In the case of the airline industry, however, Korean Air directly regulates the activities of foreign airlines serving South Korea.

One of the techniques historically used by industry associations to control the behavior of foreign competitors was to enact non-tariff barriers that made it difficult or impossible for the foreign firms to do business—a situation that the South Korean government has been working to resolve, with some success.

The Prime Contact for Newcomers

The most important contact for any foreign company proposing to do business in or with South Korea is the American Chamber of Commerce (AmCham) in Seoul. The chamber is a strong, vocal advocate on behalf of foreign business, and has accumulated a substantial amount of information and insight on the laws, regulations, and subtleties of doing business in the country.

Among the 32 chamber member committees that contribute to these insights are banking, financial services, intellectual property, joint ventures, labor, living and civil affairs, ROK government liaison, taxation and the U.S. Government, trade expansion, and transportation.

The chamber sponsors briefing meetings for individual companies on a monthly basis, providing newcomers with the insights and guidance of a number of old-timers who have learned the ropes, often the hard way, through years of experience in South Korea.

Depending on the kind of business you want to do in South Korea, the AmCham can direct you to other sources of information and help, from the commercial section of the U.S. Embassy and branches of foreign banks to appropriate South Korean government agencies and offices.

Direct enquiries should be made to:

American Chamber of Commerce in Korea
#4501, Trade Tower 159-1
Samsung-dong,
Kangnam-Ku,
Seoul 135-729
Korea
Tel: (82-2) 564-2040
Fax: (82-2) 564-2050
E-mail: amchamrsvp@amchamkorea.org
www.amchamkorea.org

The Good Side

Despite the many cultural and political handicaps involved in doing business in South Korea, there are even more compensations that make the effort worthwhile for a growing number of foreign businesses. On a personal level, South Koreans are a sincere, warm, and friendly people who have often been described as "the Irish of the Orient." They make deep commitments of friendship and loyalty that are permanent if they are treated fairly and with respect. By the same token, if they are mistreated, they make formidable enemies.

It is the personal quality of life and relationships in South Korea that attracts so many Westerners to persevere in the face of professional and political obstacles. They come to love and admire Koreans and become greatly attached to many aspects of the culture.

In a strictly business context, the ROK represents a large market, with a highly disciplined workforce, few labor problems, a high standard of education, an overwhelming ambition to better itself economically and socially, and ever rising expectations.

A significant percentage of South Korea's top managers were educated in the United States. They not only speak English well, but they are especially friendly toward the United States. These foreign-educated Koreans in particular are imbued with an extraordinary "can do" spirit that is exciting and catching, and augurs well for South Korea.

Another special advantage that foreigners have in South Korea is that Koreans feel at ease with foreigners. Unlike the average Japanese, they do not find associating with or dealing with foreigners an emotional burden, and are therefore able to deal more effectively with non-Koreans. Japanese businessmen continuously comment on how tiring and nerve-racking it is for them to be in close contact with Westerners, even when they (the Japanese) speak English fairly well. South Koreans, on the other hand, seem to thrive on associating with foreigners and are much more aggressive and forthcoming in their relationships.

Koreans are very conscious of their long history and the great artistic achievements of their civilization. This consciousness has been translated into official government policy, which mandates that the cultural heritage of the country be protected and incorporated in the national infrastructure. This concern for, and use of, art adds a special ambience to life in South Korea that is growing more common and significant with each passing year. It adds to the attraction of living and working in South Korea, and is a definite plus for the growing foreign community.

A Pending Retirement Law

As of this writing (June 2013), if a law proposed by the South Korean government goes into effect it will have a fundamental impact on Western companies operating in the country. At present many Korean companies have a mandatory retirement age of 55, and some force out employees who are even younger to make room for new recruits.

The proposed new law would set the retirement age at 60, which sounds like an improvement, but it leaves foreign companies up in the air about employees who are in their sixties and seventies and represent their most experienced and often most valuable employees.

CHAPTER FIVE

Vocabulary of the Korean Way

achom (ah-choam)—It is very important in South Korea to maintain a positive, friendly demeanor and avoid hurting anyone's feelings. Part of this process consists of the generous use of compliments and flattery, or *achom*. Foreigners not familiar with the social custom are likely to confuse such flattery and compliments with extraordinary politeness, and a friendly, easygoing, cooperative attitude. While the latter may be true in individual situations, the practice of *achom* has a far more serious purpose. Also see *kibun*.

amukuto anida (ah-muu-kuu-toe ah-nee-dah)—This is a common response when someone in South Korea is given a hard task. It means, "It's nothing, I can do it easily," and is indicative of the "can do" spirit of South Koreans.

apatu (ah-pah-tuu)—The size and location of an *apatu* (apartment) is of special importance in South Korea because it is associated with social class, which in turn is an important factor in the type of work one is able to obtain and where one works. Foreign managers in South Korea should be aware of the class factor and take it into account in their dealings and relationships with South Korean employees.

bokshin (boak-sheen)—*Bokshin* refers to an aide or assistant who is so trusted by the boss that he is allowed to act on his behalf. The literal meaning of the term is, roughly, "man in his belly."

bural an chok (buu-rahl ahn choak)—A man who builds up a business enterprise with hard work but little capital is said to have done it *bural an chok*, or "only with balls."

byul jang (buul jahng)—Literally a "remote house," this is the Korean word for a recreational villa, usually on the coast or in the mountains. Many of the *byul jang* in South Korea are maintained by large companies for their employees.

chaebol (chay-bowl)—This is the term used for South Korea's huge business-industrial complexes, such as Hyundai, Samsung, LG (formerly Lucky and Goldstar), and the SK Group. It is the Korean equivalent of the well-known Japanese term *zaibatsu*.

chagayong unjonsa (chah-gah-yong uun-joan-sah)— Just as in other countries, personal chauffeurs (*chagayong unjonsa*) are a highly prized status symbol in South Korea. They are especially practical for businessmen who work in the downtown areas of Seoul and other major South Korean cities, because of the scarcity of parking places.

chakupjachok (chah-kuup-jah-choke)—The "self-sufficiency syndrome." Given Korea's historical circumstance, divided by exclusive clans and by regional kingdoms that were usually in conflict with each other, as well as being surrounded by countries that were hostile and invaded and occupied the whole peninsula several times, it was natural for Koreans on all levels—from individual families to the highest elite—to attempt to be as self-sufficient as possible. This self-sufficiency syndrome, expressed in the Korean term *chakupja-chok* (chah-kuup-jah-choke), was the driving force behind attempts by companies in South Korea in the aftermath of World War II to grow into huge combines that did everything—from controlling the raw materials they needed to the retailing process. (It also became the mantra of North Korea's isolated Communist leaders.)

Foreign companies dealing with South Korea invariably run into the self-sufficiency concept, which remains a primary factor in the policies and practices of the government, because the country's leaders are determined that South Korea will never again come under the political or economic hegemony of any outside power.

That said, both government and business leaders now understand that South Korea must continue the globalization process of their economy in order to continue to fulfill the potential of its people and contribute to the peace and prosperity of the world. Both businesspeople and diplomats involved with South Korea should be prepared to deal with this powerful syndrome.

chehan (chay-hahn)—This is the word for "restriction," which is often used in South Korea, particularly in relation to imports and exports.

chibaein (chee-by-een)—South Koreans take such titles as *chibaein* (manager) very seriously, and it is common to address them by their titles instead of by their names, particularly since so many people have the same family name (in a company with one hundred employees, as many as ten or more may be named Lee, another ten or so may be named Pak, and there may be ten or more Kims, etc.).

chido (chee-doe)—This is the Korean equivalent of the Japanese term *shido*, which is used in connection with government "guidance" of industry. It is somewhat less commonly used in South Korea because there is very little effort to disguise or deny that the government's role is more in the nature of control than guidance.

chim shin uro (cheem sheen uu-roe)—The Korean term for "pure heart," this is used in reference to a person of impeccable integrity and sincerity who can be depended upon to do what is right. It is a quality South Korean employers pay special attention to when hiring.

chinchok (cheen-choke)—Korea's strong family orientation extends well beyond the nuclear family to include relatives (*chinchok*) that are two, three, and four times removed. This sometimes complicates their relationships with Westerners. The foreigner who marries a Korean is often surprised at the size of the "family" he or she has acquired (and is obligated to).

chip an (cheep ahn)—The Korean equivalent of the Japanese *uchi*, which is used in the sense of "my house," "my home," "my company." *Chip an* literally means "inside the house" and is used in the same way as the Japanese word. The usage indicates the close relationship Koreans develop with their place of employment, putting it on the level of their home.

chisongnyok (chee-song-nyoke)—This is the term used by Koreans in reference to their incredible capacity to endure physical and mental stress. It is seen as one of their major national strengths.

chohoe (choe-hay)—The "morning meeting" or "morning ceremony" (*chohoe*) has been adopted by most major South Korean companies, and the practice is growing. The *chohoe* held by some companies is very ceremonial—in some the national anthem is played.

chongchi (chong-chee)—Politics (*chongchi*) plays some role in almost every foreign business deal consummated in South Korea, so this is a useful word to know. Another important word is *chongbu*, meaning "government."

chongddae (chong-dday)—Literally "the barrel of a gun," this is the South Korean version of "hired gun," or someone who does an unpleasant job for the boss.

chongui (chong-we)—The Korean concept of justice (*chongui*) is based more on what is agreed to be good for society and the country than on what is best for the individual. Because of this philosophical difference, foreigners who become involved in court cases in South Korea are often disappointed with the outcome.

chongyong (chone-gyong)—Because of the vertical structure of their society and the importance of maintaining and protecting one's social status, South Koreans are very sensitive about paying and being paid proper respect (*chongyong*). Foreigners living and working in South Korea must learn something about this etiquette and make use of it in order to function effectively.

chonmae (chone-my)—The South Korean government operates a number of monopolies (*chonmae*) as a method of earning income. The monopolized products include ginseng and tobacco.

chonmae tuko (chone-my tuu-kah)—In South Korea, foreign patents (*chonmae tuko*) must be registered in both Korean and the language of the originating country.

chonmun-ga (chone-muun-gah)—While the idea of paying a consulting fee or a royalty to someone for their advice or the use of their intellectual achievements used to be foreign to Koreans, they now recognize the value of *chonmun-ga*, or

"experts," and make use of a growing number of foreign consultants, engineers, and scientists.

chuchon (chuu-chone)—A *chuchon*, or "recommendation," is
very important in making new contacts in South Korea. The
recommendation may be written or verbal. The best is verbal
and in person.

chukcheil (chuke-chay-eel)—Folk festivals (*chukcheil*), many
of them dating from before recorded history and shamanistic in origin, continue to play a vital role in the lives of most
South Koreans. They are especially important events in rural
areas.

chulhyong sawon (chule-hyong sah-woan)—This is a "worker
or employee on loan" to an affiliated or subsidiary firm. It
generally carries the connotation that it is a temporary
situation, but the transfer may also be permanent. Valued
employees are often sent out to help rescue smaller, affiliated
companies that have gotten into trouble. It is also a common
practice when one company acquires another firm, either to
control it or to assist its management.

chusik hoesa (chuu-sheek hoe-eh-sah)—A "stock company."
This is the most common type of company organization in
South Korea.

daedulpo (day-duul-poe)—Literally "stone and pillar." Figuratively, this refers to the person in an office, agency, or company who is primarily responsible for keeping it going and
for its success. "Stone" refers to a foundation stone, and
"pillar" to what holds a building up; hence the "backbone"
of the company.

daepochip (day-poe-cheep)—This is the Korean equivalent of
the Japanese word *akachin* (ah-kah-cheen), or red lantern,
symbolic of drinking and drinking establishments. However,

the literal meaning of *daepochip* is something like "house of artillery," or a place where big guns are kept. The inference is that when people drink they often shoot off their mouths. The more they drink, the bigger the "shots" they fire. Red lanterns are not hung in front of South Korean drinking places as they are in Japan.

danyom hada (dahn-yoam hah-dah)—This is the Korean equivalent of "throwing in the towel" or giving up or dropping something, such as negotiations that are not going anywhere or a product that is losing money. The literal translation is something like "cutting one's mind."

dollah box (dollar box)—A company's most profitable product, line, or department is frequently referred to as its "dollar box." A company's source of financing may also be called this.

dong chang saeng (dong chahng sang)—A South Korean businessman's biggest asset is his *dong chang saeng*, or "network," made up of classmates, alumni brothers, friends from the military, relatives, relations by marriage, and other close friends he has made along the way. The foreign businessman must take the same approach, developing his own network.

dulinda (duu-leen-dah)—This is a commonly used greeting among businesspeople in South Korea when they make courtesy calls on customers or contacts. It means, more or less, "Are you at peace?" in reference to the fact that Korea has experienced so much warfare in its history. The present-day meaning is something like, "Are things going well?"

gara mungeida (gah-rah muun-gay-dah)—Literally "to crush with one's rear end," this is the equivalent of killing a proposal or application by sitting on it, something that government bureaucrats in South Korea and elsewhere are often accused of.

hachong (hah-chong)—All of South Korea's large, well-known companies have a network of *hachong* (subcontract firms) beneath them. Just as in Japan and other countries, the subcontract firms are used as cushions to shield the major companies from fluctuations in demand, prices, and exchange rates.

haengjong (hang-joang)—While generally following Confucian principles, the *haengjong*, or "administration," in South Korean companies is often significantly affected by the personal style of the president or chairman, and when several members of the same family are involved in top management.

hakuksang (hah-kuuk-sahng)—In South Korea's tightly structured vertical society, *hakuksang*, or "going over a superior's head," is a very serious matter. Management ranks in larger companies are as clearly defined and as guarded as those in the military.

Hangugo (Hahn-guu-go)—The Korean language.

Hanguk (hahn-gook)—This is the Korean word for "Korea." It means "Great Country." The word for "Korean person" is *Hangug-in* (hahn-goog-een).

Hanguk umshik (hahn-gook uum-sheek) or *hanshik* (hahn-sheek)—This is the term for "Korean food," which the visitor will find very useful. If you don't want to eat Korean food every day, it is also advisable to learn how to say *yang shik* (foreign food).

Hangul (hahn-guul)—The Korean system of writing—the special phonetic characters used to write the language—was developed by a team of scholars in the early 1400s at the request of King Sejong. It is the only writing system known to have been deliberately designed by a group of experts over a short period of time. The symbols can be learned in a day or so, as opposed to the many months or years required to learn the ideograms used in Japan and China, and to a lesser and decreasing degree in South Korea.

hanjan hapshida (Hahn-jahn hop-she-dah)—A commonly heard term in South Korea's business world, this is the equivalent of "let's have a drink." It is rare, however, for the guest to get by with having only one drink. South Korean businessmen tend to put as much enthusiasm and energy into drinking as they do working.

hanjan man (hahn jahn mahn)—Meaning "only one glass," this is the common South Korean invitation used to invite someone out for a drink and a talk, usually after business hours. "One glass" should not be taken literally.

hapcha Hoesa (hop-chah hoe-eh-sah)—A limited partnership company.

hapmyng hoesa (Hop-ming hoe-eh-sah)—A partnership company, a form of company organization that is rare in South Korea.

hoegyesa (Hoag-yay-sah)—The *hoegyesa*, or accountant, in a South Korean firm is an important individual. It can be very helpful for the foreign businessman to establish a strong personal relationship with the *hoegyesa*.

huisaeng ta (hwee-sang tah)—Literally a "sacrifice batter," this is a person sent in to learn as much as possible before serious negotiations start, or used some other way as a frontman who plays an early but limited role to gain a fast advantage.

hukmak (huke-mahk)—It is common in South Korea for an individual behind the scenes (*hukmak*) to be the one who really exercises power. *Hukmak* means "black curtain." Another term also used is *makhu shil yokja* (mahk-huu sheel yoakjah), which means "strong man behind a curtain."

hwandae (hwahn-die)—This is the word for Korea's famous hospitality, which can be overwhelming, but pays off in the goodwill and cooperation that it generates.

hwanyong hoe (whan-yong hay)—South Koreans are noted for their elaborate *hwanyong hoe*, or "welcoming receptions," which are part of their custom of conspicuous hospitality. They are customary when welcoming new employees into a company, and when formally greeting newly arrived guests, especially from abroad.

hyongshikchogin (h'yong-sheek-choe-gheen)—South Korean businessmen and government officials tend to be *hyongshik-chogin* (formal) in their behavior, especially toward foreign guests.

hyopoe (hyahp-po-eh)—Associations (*hyopoe*) are a vital aspect of business as well as personal affairs in South Korea. Generally speaking, many of the associations dealing with business constitute obstacles to foreign companies operating in South Korea, since they are exclusive and are designed to give the South Korean members an advantage over foreign companies.

Ilbonsaram (eel-bone-sah-rahm)—This word means "Japanese person," and is something Koreans do not like to be mistaken for. Generally speaking, Korean men are physically larger and more muscular than Japanese, and the women are taller and have larger busts and wider hips than their Japanese counterparts.

ilbulrae (eel-buul-ray)—"Working like an insect" is the Korean equivalent of a workaholic. The term is used often, generally in a positive, complimentary way. As one man said, "In Korea, the person who works like a bee is respected."

inhwa (inn-whah)—One of the key principles of traditional

Korean society, *inhwa* means "harmony," in this case, based on Confucian concepts of hierarchical relationships between people, respect for elders, obedience to authority, coordinated group behavior, and decisions by consensus.

in maek (inn make)—These are the personal connections that are so essential to both private and business life in South Korea. Instead of starting from the objective and moving to the subjective, as is common in the West, virtually all relationships in South Korea start with the subjective or personal side. The importance of these personal connections is suggested by the term *in maek*, which means something like "human pulse."

ipto ssagi (eep-toe sah-ghee)—This refers to the practice of hiring high school or university students before they graduate, in order to get the pick of the crop. The word literally means "standing rice," and originally referred to brokers buying rice before it was harvested. It is also used in reference to buying stocks or merchandise before it has been made or while it is still in the factory.

jaebul (jay-buul)—Many companies in South Korea belong to a specific *jaebul*, or group, and in various ways coordinate their operations with the leading firms heading up their groups. *Jaebul* is also used in reference to financial groups.

jajunggu bakwi dolligi (jahjuung-guu bahk-we dole-leeghee)—A person who is being given the runaround by a company or government agency is said to be *jajunggu bakwi dolligi* or "pedaling a stationary bike." In other words, he isn't going anywhere.

jal butak hamnida (jahl buu-tock hahm-nee-dah)—One of the most used phrases in the Korean language, this means something like "please do whatever you can for me." It is said to people when you want them to take care of something or do something, whether it is a favor or something they are obligated to do anyway. It is an institutionalized, stock phrase, and is the equivalent of Japan's *yoroshiku onegaishimasu*. It is used in both informal and formal situations, and is a way of humbling yourself so the other person won't regard your request as arrogant.

jang ki (jahng kee)—Koreans take great pride in their ability to sing or perform some other kind of entertaining skill, which they are regularly called upon to do at parties. They generally practice these skills in private, a custom that is called *jang ki*, or "favorite technique."

jimmu kyuchik (jeem-muu kyu-cheek)—"Company rules," something every foreign company in South Korea should have, and should require all new employees to sign as one of the conditions of employment.

joja sei (joejah-say-e)—It has historically been dangerous for individual Koreans to stand out in a crowd or to draw attention to themselves when things go wrong or there is any kind of problem. Under these circumstances, it is common for them to *joja sei*, or "lay low." This can, and often does, cause additional problems in a company when keeping quiet compounds the situation.

joong-in (joong-inn)—The *joong-in*, or upper-middle class, during Korea's long feudal period was made up mostly of professionals, including doctors, lawyers, translators, and middle-ranked military officers. The same groups are prominent in today's society, but are no longer hereditary or so clearly defined.

junggi chaeyong (juung-ghee chay-yong)—This means "periodic hiring," and refers to the custom of South Korean companies hiring high school and university graduates in batches in March, when the school year ends.

jupan i anmaja (juu-pahn ee ahn-mahjah)—When Koreans feel that a price is too high, they are likely to say *jupan i anmaja* or that their "abacus is unbalanced."

jwachon (jwah-choan)—Literally a "change to the left," this term refers to someone being demoted or transferred to a job with less prestige. It comes from the old custom of seating inferiors on the left.

kanpan (kahn-pahn)—This is the Korean equivalent of the famous Japanese word *kanban*, which originally meant "sign" or "bulletin board," but now refers to the "just-in-time" delivery system made famous by Japanese manufacturers. South Korean companies adapted the system to their own manufacturing process. The name originated from the practice initiated by a manager of Toyoda Loom Works of having a big overhead sign posted in the factory listing the parts that were to be delivered that day. Toyoda Loom Works was the forerunner of Toyota Motors Corporation.

keiyul hoesa (kay-e-yuul hay-sah)—South Korean companies are generally "aligned" with one of the major *chaebol* groups, and are known as *keiyul hoesa*, or "affiliated companies." Which group a particular company belongs to can have a significant influence on its overall business, from its ability to raise capital to how effectively it can distribute and promote products in the South Korean market. Foreign companies contemplating going into business with South Korean firms should identify and familiarize themselves with their group affiliations.

keo mul (kay-oh muul)—A man of exceptional power and influence is often referred to as a *keo mul*, or "big shot."

kibu (kee-buu)—Surprisingly, one of the "problems" of doing business in South Korea is the pressure brought on companies to make frequent and sizeable *kibu* (donations) for causes that range from the very worthwhile to the very obscure and doubtful. It is often advisable to investigate groups soliciting donations before parting with your money. Even legitimate organizations tend to overdo it, however.

kioe chae yong (kee-way chay yong)—This phrase means "hiring out-of-season," or the practice of hiring new employees at times other than following graduation, when most companies do their annual hiring.

ko e kulmyun (koe ee kuul-me-uun), or *gui e kulmyun* (gwee ee kuul-me-uun)—These two terms mean "nose ring" and "earring," and are used in reference to a situation or thing (such as a contract) that can be interpreted in two or more ways, or a person who changes his attitude or position to suit the circumstances.

kolpu (kole-puu)—This is Korean for "golf," an activity that is seen by South Korean businessmen as an important part of international socializing.

komun (koe-muun)—A Korean *komun* (consultant or advisor), especially one of high social standing with important government and industry contacts, can be invaluable to foreign companies wanting to do business in South Korea. Retired government officials from key ministries as well as company executives from leading firms are also much in demand for their knowledge and network of contacts.

Kongja (kong-jah)—This is the Korean word for Confucius, perhaps the most important figure in Korean history. Familiarity with the primary teachings of Confucius is a great asset in understanding the attitudes and customs of South Koreans.

kongson (kong-soan)—Politeness (*kongson*), combined with Confucian-style respect, is one of the primary facets of the Korean social system. South Koreans tend to be very formal in business and official relations. Generally speaking, businessmen, government officials, and other professionals in the company of foreigners relax completely only during nighttime drinking parties.

korae (koe-rye)—Given the extraordinary compulsion South Koreans have for bettering themselves, and the equally competitive nature of the economy, smaller independent businessmen are constantly on the lookout for *korae*, or business deals. Their enthusiasm is so great it frequently outstrips their ability to perform. Newcomers should be aware of this factor, and be sufficiently thorough in checking out potential business partners.

kukche kyohon (kook-chay k'yoe-hoan)—International marriages (*kukche kyohon*), particularly between American men and South Korean women, have been fairly common-place since the early 1950s, when the U.S. began stationing large numbers of troops and civilian workers there. South Korean women have been renowned for ages for their beauty, strength, loyalty, and other sterling qualities—to the extent that they were once regarded as one of the reasons why neighboring nations were motivated to conquer South Korea.

kukpiui (kook-pee-we)—Korean people's family-oriented outlook also extends to companies, so they do not think of such things as personal problems, financial affairs, and the like as matters to be treated as confidential (*kukpiui*). This cultural characteristic often upsets foreigners, who are not accustomed to what they see as private issues being openly discussed, particularly matters concerning wages, bonuses, and sensitive deals.

kye (keh)—Cooperation and Mutual Help Pools. There is a deeply engrained personal and family aspect to doing business in South Korea that is based on the pooling of funds and work to accomplish tasks and start new businesses.

These mutual help groups get involved in such things as raising money to help celebrate auspicious birthdays of parents,
planning and staging weddings, paying for funerals, financing new businesses, and running "lottery pools" for wives.

All of these group efforts come under the word *kye*
(keh), which means something like "agreement" or "bond."
Foreign businesspeople stationed in South Korea can win
considerable merit by making themselves aware of *kye* programs among their friends and employees, and making some
kind of contribution to them.

kyesanso (kay-sahn-soe)—This is the kind of bill or check one
gets in a restaurant, which frequently results in a tug-of-war
or a flurry of arm-wrestling with fellow Korean diners, who
will frequently try to take the bill by force and pay it. Many
foreigners who are subjected to this physical assault give up
the struggle fairly quickly, out of embarrassment, even when
they know it is their place to pay.

kyeyak (kay-yahk)—Because of the personal nature of the business system in South Korea, a *kyeyak*, or contract, may be
regarded as a personal arrangement between the individuals
who signed it. This makes it extremely important for foreign
companies to establish and maintain close personal relations
with all levels of management in the South Korean firms they
deal with.

kyonbon (kyoan-bone)—Much to the surprise and dismay of
foreign businessmen, South Korean customs and excise often
charge duties on product samples (*kyonbon*). Customs officials have a considerable amount of personal discretion in
whether or not duties are charged, and at what rate.

kyongjaeng (kyong-jang)—Competition (*kyongjaeng*) is a way
of life in South Korea. There is intense rivalry for the best
education, the best job, the best of everything. Competition
occurs on an individual, family, group, or company basis, as

well as at a national level (especially in international sports competitions). It is one of the reasons for the remarkable economic advances made by South Korea since the 1960s.

kyosop (k'yoe-sop)— Koreans are skilled at negotiation (*kyo-sop*), in part because theirs is a very emotional culture with a highly refined verbal etiquette that makes it necessary for everyone to develop the ability to speak effectively, to manipulate the feelings of others, and to win by persuasion.

kyoyuk (k'yoe-yuke)—South Koreans are compulsive about getting an education (*kyoyuk*) because it has traditionally been one of the principal criteria for determining social class and advancement. For much of their long feudal history, which actually did not end until 1945, only members of the hereditary upper class could aspire to a higher education and to positions of authority. Now that education is open to all, and access to the official power structure is still decided on the basis of education, South Korean parents go to extreme lengths to see that their children get the best possible education, with the greatest achievement being several years of postgraduate study in the United States.

maeddugi hanchul (may-duu-ghee hahn-chuul)—This refers to the seasons when retail outlets are the busiest and make the most profits. The term literally means "grasshopper season," from the fact that during the short harvest season in Korea grasshoppers eat with an intense frenzy, knowing that the food supply will disappear with the coming cold.

mal i manta (mahl ee mahn-tah)—"Many words" or "one who talks too much," is used in reference to a person who attempts to use logic over feelings, or cold reason over personal considerations. In Korea, people who try to use logic all the time and do a lot of talking are generally regarded with disdain, since this goes against the grain of a society based on human and personal feelings.

mansei (mahn-say)—This is the Korean equivalent of the Japanese *banzai* cry, but its use is slightly different. In South Korea it is most often used at sporting events when someone wins or does something spectacular. In business it is customarily used to celebrate the signing of a contract or the accomplishment of an especially difficult task. It is a shout expressing pleasure and joy on an auspicious occasion. The closest English equivalent is "Hip! Hip! Hooray!"

mitopop (meet-tah-pop)—This is Korean for the "metric system," which is standard in South Korea.

mogaji (moe-gah-jee)—This is an old way of expressing the concept of dismissing or firing someone. It literally means "to cut off one's head"—*mogaji taranada*—upon which the head flies away.

mojo (moe-joe)—Shoppers in South Korea are often advised to be wary of imitation gems (*mojo posok*), but copies (*mobang*) of famous-brand products are more common than fake gems.

mok (moke)—Some South Korean imports and exports are often controlled by government-dispensed quotas (*mok*) based on the previous year's performance. This system has allowed individual companies to monopolize some import and export categories.

mumohan (muu-moe-hahn)—Koreans are noted for their hospitality, which often verges on the extreme and derives from a compelling urge to both please and impress. This behavior gives the impression that they are unreasonably *mumohan*, or "extravagant" by nature, often to their own detriment. But when others are conditioned to the same custom it all balances out.

munan kanda (muun-ahn kahn-dah)—This is an institutionalized expression used by people of an equal or lower rank when inquiring about how things are going with them. It means "go and ask if someone is at peace" (because historically there were so many clan wars in Korea).

munhwa (muun-whah)—Koreans are very proud of their *munhwa*, or culture, and this pride is an important part of their nationalism, their attitudes toward foreigners, and their treatment of foreign businessmen. Foreign visitors and residents in South Korea are expected to exhibit suitable interest in the cultural accomplishments of the country, and to respect both cultural artifacts and laws that mandate a cultural component in many business decisions.

myungmul (me-yung-muul)—Each of the major geographical areas in South Korea has a certain number of *myungmul*, or "famous products," for which it has been noted for centuries. The items are popular gifts and souvenirs among Koreans traveling from other areas.

nat dungjang (naht duung-jahng)—Literally "day lamp," this term is a derogatory reference to people in companies— often managers and executives—who do very little work and appear to make little or no contribution to their departments—much as lights left on during the day.

noryon-ga (no-ree-own-gah)—Because of their long history of venerating scholarship and knowledge, Koreans have a great deal of respect for true experts (*noryon-ga*). This has proven to be a significant advantage to foreign professionals associated with South Korean companies.

ockji (oak-jee)—A familiar phrase in the Korean business lexicon, *ockji* means "I'll do it anyway" when given a task that appears to be impossible.

ondanghan (own-dahng-hahn)—The Korean concept of *ondanghan*, or "fair," often differs from the Western interpretation because it is not necessarily an absolute principle, and changes with circumstances. For example, many South Koreans believe it is unfair for the U.S. to expect reciprocal access to its market, which is much smaller and more vulnerable than the North American market.

ondol (own-dole)—Sometime before the first century B.C., Koreans developed a central radiant heating system to warm their homes and buildings during the cold winter months— more than 2,000 years before central heating was to become common anywhere else in the world. The system consisted of running pipes beneath the floors of buildings and forcing the heat from wood-burning stoves to circulate through the pipes. People sat and slept on mats on the warm floors. The *ondol* system is still common in some rural areas of South Korea. Modern multi-level apartments use water heated by furnaces.

oryo u shijiman (oh-ree-yoe uu shejee-mahn)—Another institutional phrase that is used often in South Korea, this means in essence: "I know it is difficult but please do your best (to do me a favor or help me get something done)."

pangsongmang (pahng-song-mahng)—The nature of Korean society has resulted in the use of *pangsongmang*, or networks, as the primary form of mutual help and cooperation in both private matters and in business. The institutionalized networks include the extended family, school classmates, people born in the same village or town, and friends made while serving in the military and while working for the same government agencies or ministries.

piso (pee-soe)—Foreign managers working in South Korea are advised to hire their own private secretaries (*piso*)—as opposed to allowing a joint-venture partner or someone else to hire them—in order to ensure a greater degree of loyalty and obligation.

poikotu (poy-kot-tuu)—Because of national and cultural cohesiveness, South Koreans are often able to act together for popular causes in a way that is the envy of such poly-cultural countries as the United States. One instance of this are boycotts (*poikotu*) against the products of countries that offend them. On other occasions, said one South Korean business executive, "We simply order our wives and family not to buy certain products."

ponggonjogin (pong-gahnjoe-gheen)—Some of the social and political tenets of South Korea are still basically *ponggonjogin* (feudal), and often interfere with the attempts of the South Koreans to fully adopt a democratic form of government and society. Feudalistic thinking continues to play a role in the management of some government offices and companies.

ponosu (poe-no-suu)—The twice-a-year bonus (*ponosu*) has become an integral part of the income of company employees in South Korea. Companies are often called on to pay bonuses even when profits do not warrant them. This is done to avoid disappointing and angering employees as well as to maintain the firm's public reputation.

pop (pap)—South Korean law (*pop*) is said to be much more like German law than American law, and is therefore difficult for Americans to understand and appreciate. There is also a strong tendency to interpret the law from both a Confucian and nationalistic viewpoint.

posu (poe-suu)—It is often said that South Koreans work for bosses (*posu*) instead of companies (the opposite of the Japanese), because of the deep personal bonds that are essential for Koreans to maintain a successful relationship, whether privately or in business. As a result, Korean workers often display more loyalty to their immediate bosses than to their employers.

puha (puu-hah)—The role of the *puha*, or "follower," in South Korea companies is of vital importance, especially when the chairman of the board or the president decides to step down. In most cases, company heads are regarded as dynasties in which the retiring leader has the right to name his successor, often his most faithful follower or the one whom he thinks is most likely to continue his philosophy and policies.

puin (puu-een)—Another person's wife. Also called *ojumoni* (oh-juu-moe-nee).

pumjil (pume-jeel)—With their long history as manufacturers of handicrafts that long ago achieved the *pumjil* (quality) of fine arts, Koreans have a cultural sense of, and natural desire for, both good design and quality in all of their products. These deeply entrenched traits were a major factor in the rapid emergence of South Korea as an exporting nation.

pyong (p'yong)—One *pyong* is a specific measurement of 3.3 square meters, and is used to describe the size of plots of land, the floor space of buildings, etc. The number of *pyong* in a person's home is also used as a measure of their social status.

pyonhosa (pyone-hoe-sah)—There are relatively few *pyonhosa* (attorneys) in South Korea because the Korean concept of personal and business relations generally precludes their use in settling disputes or negotiating business or financial deals. South Korean executives who were educated abroad are, of course, much more comfortable with the use of attorneys in their business dealings.

rotori (roe-tah-ree)—This is the Korean pronunciation of "rotary," which refers to a traffic circle. For some reason, there are many rotaries in Seoul, and until you get used to them they can make driving in the city very confusing.

sahun (sah-huun)—Virtually all large South Korean companies

have their own *sahun*, or slogans and "company instructions." Most of the slogans and statements represent the
personal philosophies of the founders. In some South Korean
companies, these precepts are read aloud at morning meetings and on special occasions.

sangmin (sahng-meen)—The lower-middle class in feudal Korea
(*sangmin*) was made up of artists, craftsmen, fishermen,
farmers, and merchants.

sangpyo (sahng-pyoe)—South Korean consumers are very *sangpyo*, or brand-conscious. Those who can afford it often prefer to buy famous international brands, even when equivalent
South Korean-made products are available.

sapyo (sah-pee-yoe)—It is rare for South Korean employees
to leave a large, well-known company. When they do, most
write *sapyo*, or formal resignation letters, stating their reasons. If the employee is considered valuable by top management, considerable effort may be made to persuade him to
remain with the company.

sasaenghwal (sah-sang-whal)—The concept of *sasaenghwal*,
or privacy, is not nearly as explicit or as valued in South
Korea as it is in much of the West. Because of the communal
nature of life during their long feudal period, Koreans could
have few secrets from each other. When this was combined
with the Confucian concept of suppressing individuality in
the interests of the group, a desire for personal privacy was
considered an aberration. The tendency for South Korean
employees to be unconcerned about keeping things private is
often upsetting to foreign managers.

seibei (say-bay)—At the beginning of the new business year, usually between January 3rd and 5th, it is customary for South
Korean businessmen to make courtesy calls on the directors
and presidents of their customer companies to bow and ask

for their continued patronage during the new year. This custom is known as *seibei*, or "beginning of the year bow."

seiryuk kwon (say-ee-yuke kwahn)—Literally "power place," this term refers to a favored bar or cabaret which one frequents often, is well-known by the management and staff, and therefore has "influence." Korean businessmen like to take guests, especially foreign visitors, to their *seiryuk kwon* because they are assured of special service and the guests are more likely to be impressed with them.

seoncho haget sumnida (say-own-choe hah-gate sume-nee-dah)—"I will take care of it." This commonly used phrase, when translated into English, implies that whatever the problem or request, the individual making the statement intends to literally take care of it—to come through. In the original Korean, however, this meaning is not so explicit. It means something like, "I will do my best but I'm not making any promises"—which is a very common cop-out when you have no intention of doing anything at all.

shigan-ul omsuhanun (she-ghan-ule ohm-suu-hahnuun)—Because of the strict military training most South Korean men undergo and the pace of business in South Korea, everyone tends to be very punctual (*shigan-ul omsuhanun*), and expects the same of others.

shihom (she-home)—*Shihom*, or "examinations," are a fact of life for young South Koreans. Each educational step upward is marked by increasingly difficult examinations, with the most difficult being the one to enter a prestigious university. Finally, those seeking jobs with the more desirable commercial companies and government offices must also pass tough examinations that weed out all but the brightest.

shijo (she-joe)—More so perhaps than in most countries, the *shijo* (founders) of South Korean companies tend to mold them totally from top to bottom in the image of their own management and social philosophies. One of the first things one should find out about a South Korean company is whether or not it is still headed by its founder, and if so, to obtain as deep an understanding as possible of his personal beliefs and policies.

shikunbap (she-kuun-bahp)—"Cold food." When an individual in a company or a government office or agency is shunted off the promotional ladder, an obvious sign that he is not going to reach the higher executive levels, he is sometimes described as being fed *shikunbap*, or cold food. Most such people lose much of their power or influence within the company, since everyone knows they are not going to advance in the managerial hierarchy. Foreign businessmen approaching South Korean companies should try to make sure they have not been passed off to a "cold food eater."

shimalseo (she-mahl-say-oh)—A *shimalseo* is a "letter of apology," often written following some kind of problem as an official expression of regret aimed at repairing damaged relations.

shimushik (she-muu-sheek)—On the first day of business after the New Year holidays, South Korean companies generally hold *shimushik*, or "starting business ceremonies," to mark the beginning of a new year. Executives and managers make short speeches in a festive atmosphere.

shinyong (sheen-yong)—Interpersonal as well as business relations in South Korea are based more on personal trust (*shinyong*) than on any code of ethics, philosophy, or body of law. It is therefore vital that foreign businessmen establish strong personal bonds with their South Korean agents or partners.

soju (soejuu)—A "mild" liquor made from rye, sweet potatoes, and sometimes other grains, *soju* was introduced into Korea from Mongolia in the fourteenth century. It is a clear drink, resembling vodka.

songbyul hoe (song-be-ule hay)—Such events as departing for overseas assignments are ceremoniously observed in South Korean companies by *songbyul hoe*, or "farewell parties," at which there are speeches and numerous toasts. The parties serve to strengthen personal ties among the employees and reinforce their attachment to the company.

songgum (song-gume)—There are a variety of restrictions controlling the remittance of money (*songgum*) out of South Korea. Generally speaking, the government prefers that no profits be exported from the country. It is therefore important that this facet of any joint venture be clearly approved in advance.

songsaeng (song-sang)—*Songsaeng*, or teachers, have traditionally been highly respected in Korea, where education was so important in society. The term is still one of respect, and is often applied to professionals outside of the teaching profession as a way of showing special respect. It is also sometimes used to butter-up individuals for one purpose or another. The honorific *nim*, which is the equivalent of "mister," is often added to *songsaeng*.

soryu (soe-r'yuu)—There is a contradiction in the use of *soryu* (documents) in South Korea that is often both bothersome and a detriment to business. Very few documents are created in the regular course of business. Most of the interaction between managers and personnel is verbal and few written records are kept. This often leads to misinterpretation and confusion that can be straightened out only by additional meetings. On the other hand, excessive documentation is typical of government offices and agencies, and is a special burden on businessmen.

sungshil (suung-sheel)—One of the most important words in the Korean businessman's vocabulary, *sungshil* means "sincerity" or "integrity." It is the quality employers look for in new employees, and in general is regarded as more important than technical knowledge or skill. This is also the quality South Korean businessmen first look for in their foreign contacts. They feel that without this quality in a relationship, it is better not to do business with the individual or company concerned.

tabang (tah-bahng)—Literally "tea rooms," these ubiquitous shops (there are some 35,000 of them in the country, with a quarter of these in Seoul) originally served only tea, but have evolved into the South Korean equivalent of the coffee shop and serve a wide variety of drinks and food. They come in several kinds—those catering to businessmen, to young dating couples, to the affluent "cafe-set," and to gourmet coffee lovers.

taeguk (tay-gook)—This is the national flag of South Korea. It consists of a circle made up of interlocking red and blue halves which represent the flow of the seasons, with the red or *yang* half representing the sun and the light, positive, masculine, active aspect of the cosmos; and the blue side representing the moon and the feminine, passive, cold, dark aspects of cosmic forces.

taeriin (tie-reen)—An agency (*taeriin*) is the easiest form of business relationship to establish in South Korea, but there are a number of restrictions on the activities of agents of foreign firms that must be carefully weighed before deciding on this form of representation.

taesa (tie-sah)—The position of *taesa*, or ambassador, to South Korea is an interesting assignment that is also delicate and often frustrating because of cultural factors, including the South Korean obsession-like pursuit of national economic goals. A veteran foreign ambassador in Seoul can be a valuable source of insight and information to an incoming company.

taewu (tay-wuu)—This is a word that may be used on a card to mean something like "high rank" or "senior rank" without specifying a department or position. It is primarily used to describe the kind of service given to VIPs and special guests. Visiting businessmen are often given this kind of treatment (and thereafter feel obligated to their hosts and inclined to be less demanding in their business negotiations).

tallyok (tahl-yoak)—There are two *tallyok* (calendars) used in South Korea, the lunar calendar and the solar calendar. Holidays from both of the calendars are celebrated, so it is important for businessmen to be familiar with both.

tamye (tom-yay)—The Korean social etiquette that requires all favors and debts to be paid is known as *tamye*, which literally means "answering." This etiquette includes expressing thanks when appropriate, bowing, etc.

tanshin buin (tahn-sheen buu-een)—This term refers to employees who are transferred from their original place of employment to a branch, subsidiary, or affiliated company, often in a distant city or even foreign country, away from their families, forcing them to take care of themselves, like bachelors. The assignments are serious hardships for many older employees with families, but they are common because South Korean companies systematically transfer personnel around throughout their organizations as part of their on-the-job training.

tomping (tome-peeng)—This is "dumping," pronounced Korean style, in which the "d" and "t" sounds are often interchangeable and indistinguishable. It refers to selling goods in foreign markets at lower than production costs.

undaeng i (unn-dang ee)—The Korean word for the rear end,

undaeng i is used in a number of compounds to describe specific types of people, from those who are slow or lazy to those who are a bit strange.

yangban (yahng-bahn)—This was the upper class in feudal Korea, made up of scholar-bureaucrats (*munban*) and high-ranking military officers (*mulban*). Many South Koreans and foreign residents say the *yangban* social system still prevails, and now consists of high government bureaucrats, ranking military officers, and rich businessmen.

yeui pomjol (yay-we pahm-jahl)—The precepts of Confucianism, in which the relationships between the sexes, the young and the old, and the different social classes are carefully and minutely prescribed, are still very strong in South Korea, with the result that special attention should be given to appropriate *yeui pomjol*, or etiquette, in all personal and business relations. Generally speaking, South Korean etiquette is based on respecting one's parents and elders, on obeying superiors, on avoiding comments or behavior that would hurt the other person's feelings or harm their "face," bowing at the right time and in the right manner, saying the right things at the right time, and following age-old customs in matters relating to life's main passages—coming of age, marriage, death, etc.

yojung (yoe-juung)—This is what foreigners generally call a *kisaeng* house. *Kisaeng* actually means "hostess." *Yojung* means "inn," which in turn employs *kisaeng* to entertain its guests. *Kisaeng* are the equivalent of Japanese *geisha*—although some of them today are more like cabaret hostesses.

yonhoe (yoan-hoe-eh)—South Koreans are noted for their extravagant hospitality, especially when it comes to food. Dinners for foreign guests are almost always *yonhoe* (banquets), involving numerous courses, and a great deal of drinking.

yuhaeng (yuu-hang)—Like their Japanese neighbors, South Koreans are very *yuhaeng*, or fashion conscious, and concerned about being well-dressed. This has helped fuel the development of a large fashion industry.

yuryuk ja (yuu-ree-yuke jah)—Literally, "a person with influence," meaning someone with sufficient power or clout to make things happen, especially in reference to matters concerning the government, or getting someone a job in a desirable government agency or company. Many companies owe much of their success to having a *yuryuk ja* on their side.

Management Titles and Their Korean Equivalents

FOREIGN	KOREAN	TRANSLATION
Chairman	*Hwoe Jang*	Chairman of Board
President	*Sa Jang*	
Vice President	*Boo-Sa Jang*	
Managing Director	*Chunmoo Ee-Sa*	Principal Director
Director	*Sangmoon Ee-Sa*	Standing Director
General Manager	No equivalent	
Department Manager	*Boo Jang*	Department Chief
Assistant Dept Manager	*Cha Jang*	Vice Dept Chief
Section Manager	*Kwa Jang*	Section Chief
Assistant Section Manager	*Daeri*	Branch Chief
Senior Clerk	*Joo Im Kye Won*	Principal Job, Branch Member
Typist	*Ta Jasoo*	
Messenger	*Sa Hwan*	

Factory Titles

Factory Manager	*Kong Jang Jang*	Factory Chief
Department Manager	*Boo Jang*	Department Chief
Section Manager	*Kwa Jang*	Section Chief
Supervisor	*Daeri*	Branch Chief
Foreman	*Joo Im*	Person in Charge

Other Titles

Secretary	*Bee Seo*
Bookkeeper	*Kijangsuki*
Driver	*Oonjunsoo*

Department Names

Accounting	*Iiwegae*
Engineering	*Engineer*
General Affairs	*Chong Mu*
Machine Shop	*Keekyea Kong*
Materials	*Chache*
Material Control	*Chache Kwanree*
Plant Maintenance	*Kong Jang Sisol Kwanree*
Production	*Saengsan*
Quality Control	*Pumcheel Kwanree*
Sales	*Panmae*
Shipping/Receiving	*Balsong/Sunap*

Guide to Korean Pronunciation

Pronunciation Guide to Vowels

A	Ya	O	Yo	O
Ah	Yah	Ah	Yah	Oh
Yo	**U**	**Yu**	**U**	**I**
Yoh	Uu	Yuu	Oi	Ee

Note that the third syllable in the top line (O) is pronounced more like an "a" than an "o." For example *oje* ("yesterday") is pronounced "ay-jay." *Odiso* ("where") is pronounced "ah-dee-soe." I have attempted to account for this factor in the phonetics following each word and sentence.

Pronunciation Guide to Multiple Vowels

Ae	Yae	E	Ye	Oe
Aeh	Yaeh	Eh	Yeh	Oeh
Wa	**Wo**	**Wae**	**We**	**Wi**
Wah	Wah	Wae	Weh	Wee

Pronunciation Guide for Syllables

Ka Kah	**Kya** Kyah	**Ko** Kah	**Kyo** Kyah	**Ko** Koh
Kyo Kyoh	**Ku** Kuu	**Kyu** Kyuu	**Ku** Kuu	**Ki** Kee
Na Nah	**Nya** Nyah	**No** Noo	**Nyo** Nyoe	**No** No
Nyo Nyoh	**Nu** Nuu	**Nyu** Nyuu	**Nu** Nuu	**Ni** Nee
Da Dah	**Dya** Dyah	**Do** Doe	**Dyo** Dyoe	**Do** Doe
Dyo Dyoe	**Du** Duu	**Dyu** Dyuu	**Du** Due	**Di** Dee
Ra Rah	**Rya** Ryah	**Ro** Roe	**Ryo** Ryoe	**Ro** Roe
Ryo Ryoe	**Ru** Ruu	**Ryu** Ryuu	**Ru** Rue	**Ri** Ree
Ma Mah	**Mya** Myah	**Mo** Moe	**Myo** Myoe	**Mo** Moe
Myo Myoe	**Mu** Muu	**Muu** Myuu	**Mu** Mue	**Mi** Me
Ba Bah	**Bya** Byah	**Bo** Boe	**Byo** Byoe	**Bo** Boe

Byo Byoe	**Bu** Buu	**Byu** Byuu	**Bu** Bue	**Bi** Bee
Sa Sah	**Sya** Syah	**So** Soe	**Syo** Syoe	**So** Soe
Syo Syoe	**Su** Suu	**Syu** Syuu	**Su** Sue	**Si** She
A Ah	**Ya** Yah	**O** Ohh	**Yo** Yeh	**O** Oh
Yo Yoe	**U** Yuu	**Yu** Yuu	**U** Uu	**I** Ee
Ja Jah	**Jya** Jyah	**Yo** Joe	**Jyo** Jyoe	**Jo** Joe
Jyo lyoe	**Ju** Juu	**Jyu** Juu	**Ju** Juu	**Ji** Jee
Cha Chah	**Chya** Chyah	**Cho** Choe	**Chyo** Chyoe	**Cho** Choe
Chyo Chyoe	**Chu** Chuu	**Chyu** Chyuu	**Chu** Chuu	**Chi** Chee
Ka Kah	**Kya** Kyah	**Ko** Koe	**Kyo** Hyoe	**Ko** Koe
Kyo Kyoe	**Kuu** Kuu	**Kyu** Kyuu	**Ku** Kuu	**Ki** Kee
Ta Tah	**Tya** Tyah	**To** Toe	**Tyo** Tyoe	**To** Toe

Tyo Tyoe	**Tu** Tuu	**Tyu** Tyuu	**Tu** Tue	**Ti** Tee
Pa Pah	**Pya** Pyah	**Po** Poe	**Pyo** Pyoe	**Po** Poe
Pyo Pyoe	**Pu** Puu	**Pyu** Pyuu	**Pu** Puu	**Pi** Pee
Ha Hah	**Hya** Hyah	**Ho** Hoe	**Hyo** Hyoe	**Ho** Hoe
Hyo Hyoe	**Hu** Huu	**Hyu** Hyuu	**Hu** Hue	**Hi** Hee

Index

38th Parallel 9, 43, 44

accounting, flexible 134–135
achom (compliments) 180
alphabet 24, 86
alumni groups 90
ambiguity 95, 96
American Chamber of Commerce 36, 132, 133, 176–177
ancestor worship 23
anshim ("peace of mind") 82–83
apatu (apartment) 180
apologies 173–174
appointments 118
arrogance 74
automobile production 132

baetchang ("leather belly") 150
banqueting 208
bargaining 153–154
bars and entertainment 18
behavior 48
benevolence 60
"Big Brother" 97–99, 100–101
body language, understanding 139–141
bokshin (assistant) 181
bonus 200
bowing 123–125
boycotts 199
bragging 74

bribery 121–123
broadband 11
Bronze Age 38
Buddhism 29, 39
bural an chok ("only with balls") 181
Busan 15
business clubs 18
business hours 118
Business of South Korean Culture, The (Richard Saccone) 51
byul jang ("remote house") 181

chae-myun (face saving) 77
chaebols 11–12, 13, 14, 16, 18, 133, 181, 192
chaegim (responsibility) 96–97
chakupjachok ("self sufficiency syndrome") 181–182
chambers of commerce, foreign 20–21, 36, 132, 133
chamulsong (patience) 169–170
Chang, Myun J. 44
changpi (shame) 79
chansa (compliments) 137
character, Korean 59–104
chebol (collective punishment) 171
chehan (restrictions) 182

chibaein (manager) 182
chido (government guidance of industry) 182–183
chim shin uro ("pure heart") 183
China 8, 24, 29, 38, 39, 41, 42, 108, 123
chinchok 183
Chinese language 24
chingu (friends) 101
chinshim (sincerity) 102–103
chip an ("my home") 183
chisongnyok (stress) 183
chiwi (rank) 114–115
choe (sin) 68–69
Choe Chae-sok 47
choehoe (morning meeting) 183
Choi Kyu-hah 44
chok (clans) 30–31
chol (bowing) 123–125
chongchi (politics) 184
chongddae ("the barrel of a gun") 184
chongjung (deference) 111
chongmal (truth) 83–84
chongshik 93–94
chongui (respect) 85, 184
chongyong (paying proper respect) 75, 184

chonmae (monopolies) 184

chonmun-ga ("experts") 184

chontu (public fighting) 28

Choson dynasty 22–23, 28, 29, 40–43, 49, 66, 101, 122, 163, 168

Christianity 43, 67, 68

Chrysler 132

chuchon ("recommendations") 185

chukcheil (folk festivals) 185

chulhyong sawon ("worker/employee on loan") 185

Chun Doo-hwan 45

chung (group consciousness) 49–50

chungjae ("arbitration by outsiders") 173

chungjaein (private mediator) 168, 173

chusik hoesa (stock company) 185

civil servants 133

clan wars 114, 197

clans 30–31, 114

class consciousness 89–90

class, *see* social class

cold calling 117

communication 86–88

competitiveness 109, 138, 154, 194

compliments and women 137

confidentiality 135

Confucianism 22, 25, 29, 30, 39, 40, 41, 46–47, 49, 52, 56, 62, 68, 73, 74, 76, 78, 80, 81, 84, 106, 107, 109, 110, 121, 136, 149, 173, 208

connections 142–143

consultants 21

contracts 69, 71, 127–131

"model contracts" 131

with government departments 130, 131

corporate paternalism 62

corporate philosophy 18

corruption 108

creativity 149

criticism 63, 108–109, 146

cross-cultural misunderstanding 140–141

cultural backlash 167

"cultural telepathy" 139–141

culture/cultural traits 20, 22–23, 24, 26, 27, 28–30, 31–37, 47, 54, 77, 78, 95

daedulpo ("stone and pillar") 185

Daegu 15

daepochip (drinking house) 185–186

Daewoo Group 12, 147

danranjujeom (low class business club) 18

danyom hada ("giving up") 186

decision making 147–148

defense industry 16

deference 111–112

demilitarized zone 44

Democratic Justice Party 45

dignity 146–147

dining, business 156–157

"diploma disease" 65

disobeying the law 138–139

dollah box 186

dong chang saeng (network) 186

Dredge, Dr. C. Paul 139–141

dress 119–120

drinking culture 20, 146, 155, 156, 157–160, 185, 187, 193, 204, 205

drinking partners 158

dulinda (courtesy calls) 186

duty 67–68

education 24, 65–66, 90, 91, 196

emotion 107–108, 151, 152

SEE ALSO *kamdong*

emotional needs in business 72–73, 152

emotions, extreme 57–58

English language, use of 20, 174–175

enuri (bargaining) 153

ethics 46–58, 66–67, 90, 106–110

Western 48, 68–69, 107

ethnicity 25

etiquette 29, 30, 46–58, 87–88, 90,

106–107, 115–116, 117, 142, 146–147, 184

"face" 52–53, 72, 76–80, 135, 137, 140, 146, 208
factions 113
failure, attitudes towards 18–20, 81
SEE ALSO *shilpae*
fairness, attitudes towards 88–89, 95, 107–108, 198–199
SEE ALSO *kongpyong*
family 23, 30–34, 41, 59, 74, 91, 92, 96, 145, 183
fashion 208
feudalism 23, 75, 121, 122
fighting 28
first names, use of 121
folk festivals 185
foreign chambers of commerce, SEE chambers of commerce
foreign companies 15–16, 18–20, 36–37
Foreign Investment Promotion Act 16
foreign workers 172
forms of address 115
Free Economic Zones 15
free trade zones 14
friends in business 101–102
friendship 101

gara mungeida ("to crush with one's rear end") 100, 186

gift giving 121–123
golf 193
"good mood" syndrome, SEE *kibun*
government agencies 100, 132, 133
government contracts 131, 132, 133
government offices 97–101, 126
government structure 148
Great Administration Code 40
green industry 16
greetings 123–127
SEE ALSO *insa*; *insa jang*; *sebae* and *shimushik*
group consciousness, SEE *chung*
guilt, Christian notion of 79
"guest category" 107
gyopo 20

hachong (subcontractors) 187
haengjong (administration) 187
haengjung chido ("administrative guidance") 99
hakuksang ("going over a superior's head") 187
han (resentment) 23–24
Han Yang University 147
handshake 124
Hangugo (Korean language) 86–88, 187
SEE ALSO Korean language; *Hangul*

Hanguk (Korea) 187
Hanguk umshik (Korean food) 187
Hangul (writing system) 24, 40, 86, 187–188
hanjan hapshida ("let's have a drink") 188
hanjan man ("only one glass") 188
harmony 28–30, 51, 52, 144, 190
Hideyoshi, Toyotomi 42
him 26
history, SEE Korean history
hoegyesa (accountant) 188
honor 28, 111–112, 136
SEE ALSO *myongye*
honoring superiors 111–112
hospitality 20, 78–79, 89, 146, 155–164, 187, 188, 189, 208
hukmak ("black curtain") 188
humanism 60
hwa (harmony) 28–30
hwandae (hospitality) 154–156, 189
hwanyong hoe ("welcome receptions") 189
hyopoe (associations) 100, 189
Hyundai 12

Ilbonsaram ("Japanese person") 189
ilbulrae ("working like an insect") 189

in (benevolence) 60
in make (personal connections) 190
Incheon 15
Inchon, battle 44
individualism 10–11
industrial revolution 61
Information Technology and Innovation Foundation 8, 11
in'gan kwan'gye (interpersonal relationships) 73
inhwa (harmony) 144, 189–190
injong ("compassion for others") 128
insa ("round of greetings") 126–127
insa idong (job rotation) 164–165
insa jang (written greetings) 126
integrity 67
interpersonal relationships in business 72–74
invitations 156
IPG Legal 21–22
ipto ssagi ("standing rice") 190
"irregular practices" 105–106

jaebul 190
jang ki ("favorite technique") 161, 191
Jang Song-hyon 105, 106, 166, 167, 170
Japan 10, 11, 12, 28, 41–43, 54–55, 108

Japanese invasion (1592) 42
Japanese occupation 28, 29, 43–44, 47, 59
Japanizing Korea 43
jealousy 110–111
jeol (paying respect) 74–75
jimmu kyuchik ("company rules") 165, 191
"job rotation" 164–165
joint venture operations 132–134, 139–140
joja sei ("lay low") 191
joong-in (upper-middle class) 40, 191
juche 103–104
judges 138–139
junggi chaeyong ("periodic hiring") 191
justice 84–85
SEE ALSO *chongui*
jwachon ("change to the left") 192

kamdong (emotion) 52–53
kanpan 192
keiyul hoesa (affiliated companies) 192
keo mul ("big shot") 192
Kia Motors 12
kibu (donations) 100, 192–193
kibun (feelings) 50–52, 78, 141, 180
kibun jo kye (face/manner) 52

Kim Il-sung 43, 104
Kim Jae-un 65
kindness 89
kisaeng (hostess) 160–164, 208
Koguryo kingdom 39
Kojong, king 39
kolpu (golf) 193
koman (arrogance) 53–54
komun (consultant) 193
Kongja 193
kongpyong (fairness) 56–57
kongson (courtesy) 47, 193–194
korae (business deals) 194
Korean Arbitration Board 173
Korean history 38–45
contact with Japan 41–44
early kingdoms 38–40
Korean War 44–45
last dynasty 40–41
Korean language 24, 25, 86–88
dialects 26
SEE ALSO *Hangul*
Korean Law Blog 22
Korean Trade-Investment Agency (KOTRA) 14, 16
Korean Trade-Investment Promotion Corporation 14
Korean War 8–9, 44–45, 116–117
Koryo dynasty 39
KOTRA, SEE Korean Trade-Investment Agency

kukche kyohon (international marriages) 194

kukkajuui (nationalism) 54–55

kukpiui (confidential) 194

kwalli (Korean-style management) 60–61

Kwangha 39

kye (Cooperation and Mutual Help Pools) 194–195

kyesanso (check or bill) 195

kyeyak (contract) 128, 195

kyojesul ("business drinking") 157–159

kyonbon (product samples) 195

kyong 64

kyongjaeng (competition) 154, 195–196

Kyongju 39

kyosop (negotiating) 150–151, 196

kyoyuk (education) 196

Kyung Ki High School 142

labor relations 15, 60,
language 20, 24, 25–26, 86–88, 123, 174–175
  SEE ALSO Korean language; English language, use of
law 17, 21–22, 85, 138–139, 200
lawyers 17, 21–22, 71
LG 12, 19, 144
local representatives/

go-betweens 106, 119, 133, 138, 139, 141

logic 47–49

loyalty 49–50, 62, 67, 75–76, 99, 135

Lucky and Goldstar, Inc. SEE LG

MacArthur, General Douglas 44

maeddugi hanchul ("grasshopper season") 196

male chauvinism 136–137

management Korean-style, SEE *kwalli*

management structure 142, 148–149

mangshin (shame culture) 80

manners 106–107

meeting times 118

METEC 70

military attitude 114–117, 125

military career 116–117

military regime 44–45

military service 114, 116, 171

mind control training, SEE *kyong*

Ministry of Employment and Labor 17

mitopop (metric system) 197

Mobile World Congress 8, 13

mogaji ("to cut off one's head") 197

mok (quotas) 197

morality 66–67, 107–108

moryak ("revenge plot") 110

mumohan (extravagance) 197

munhwa (culture) 198

myongye (honor) 81–82

myungmul ("famous products") 198

naekyu (unwritten laws) 100–101

name cards 33, 35, 120–21

name seals 35

names 31–36, 120, 121

naming taboos 32

National Assembly Building 140

national flag 206

nationalism 75–76, 78, 137, 144, 198
  SEE ALSO *kukkajuui*

negotiating 150–154, 195–196
  preparations 152
  success in 152

networking 145, 199

nicknames 36

noemul (bribes) 122–123

nolli (logic) 47

nollijogin 48

non drinkers 159–160

"non persons" 73

norae (singing) 160

norae bang (singing salons) 161

North Korea 8–9, 27, 43, 93, 104, 116–117, 182

Communism in 43, 104

noryon-ga (experts) 198

nunchi ("to measure with the eye") 139–141

obligation 67–68, 144–145

office call protocol 118–119

ogi ("unyielding spirit") 92–93

ondanghan ("fair") 198–199

ondol (heating system) 199

Osong 15

p'a (factions) 113

Paekche kingdom 38

pangsongmang (networks) 199

Panmunjom 44

Park Chung-hee 11, 12, 15, 44

Park Geun-hye 11

partnership companies 188

patents 184

paternalism 23, 62

patience 169–170

personal chauffeurs 181

personal relations in business 69–72, 119, 142–143, 190

personal responsibility 96–97

pipyong (criticism) 108–109

piso (private secretary) 199

poetry 23

poikotu (boycotts) 200

poksu (revenge) 109–110

ponggongjogin (feudal) 200

ponosu (bonus) 200

pop (laws) 138, 200

POSCO 12

posu (bosses) 200

"power of insight" 149–150

printing press 39

privacy, attitudes towards 73, 135, 202

private consultants 21

private secretary 199

promotions 61

public criticism 80

puha ("follower") 201

pulda ("office stress") 166

pumjil (quality) 201

pummi ("proposals submitted for deliberation") 147

punishment 171

punctuality 203

puseo jang hoe (weekly pep talks) 63

pyolmyong (nick-names) 35

pyonhosa (attorneys) 201

rank 90–91, 114–116, 124, 125

recreation 181

relationships in business 46, 47, 55, 67–68, 106, 107, 142–144

religion 28–29

resentment, SEE *han*

respect 74–76

responsibility, SEE *chaegim*

revenge 56, 109–110

reward and punish-ment 62–63

Roh Tae-woo 45

"round of greetings," SEE *insa*

Russia 43

Russo-Japanese War 1904–5 43

Saccone, Richard 51

Saddoris, John 70

sagwa (apology) 174

sahun ("company instructions") 165, 201–202

sajokuro ("personal-ism") 72

Samsung Electronics 8, 12, 13, 18, 132, 172

and Galaxy S Android phone 8, 13

sangmin 40, 202

sangpyo (brand-con-scious) 202

sapyo (formal resigna-tion letter) 202

sasaenghwal (privacy) 202

"scold management" 63

sebae ("New Year's greeting") 126–127

seibei (courtesy calls) 202–203

seiryuk kwon ("power place") 203

Sejong, king 23, 40, 86

self reliance 103–104, 181–182

self-esteem 112
senior-junior system of
  ranking 90–92
Seoul 11, 21, 44, 140,
  142, 181
Seoul National
  University (SNU) 65,
  142
servants 41
shamanism 28–29, 38,
  39
shame 53, 79–82, 102,
  109
shihom ("examina-
  tions") 203
shijo ("founders")
  203–204
shikunbap ("cold
  food") 204
shilpae 81
shimalseo ("letter of
  apology") 204
shimushik ("starting
  business ceremony")
  127, 204
Shin sang pil bol
  ("carrot and stick")
  62
shinyong (trust)
  144–145, 204
shipbuilding 11, 12
Silla kingdom 38, 39,
  160
simal ("letter of
  apology") 174
sincerity 102–103, 206
singing 160–161
singing salons 161
SK Group 12
SNU, SEE Seoul
  National University
social class 25, 27, 40,
  46, 47, 56, 73,
  89–92, 108–109,

111–114, 114–116,
  119, 122, 142
social debt 92
social hierarchy
  111–113, 114–116,
  119–120, 124–127,
  138, 142, 201
social transformation
  in South Korea
  10–11, 13
sonbae 91
songbyul hoe ("fare-
  well party") 127,
  205
Songdo 15
songgum (remittance
  of money) 205
songsaeng (teacher)
  205
songshilham (loyalty)
  76
sonnim (guests) 78
soryu (documents) 205
South Korean Business
  World 139
South Korean Strategy
  Association 139
status 25, 70–71, 73,
  89–90
stress 166
stubbornness 92–93
subcontractors 186
sulchinku ("drinking
  partners") 158
sungshil (sincerity)
  206
sunsu chida ("first to
  draw") 151
Syngman Rhee 43, 44

tabang (tea rooms) 206
taedo (manners)
  106–107
taeriin (agency) 206

taesa (ambassador)
  206–207
taewu (high rank) 207
tallyok (calendars) 207
tamye ("answering")
  207
tanga, SEE *tangol*
tangchal yok ("power
  of insight") 149–150
tangol ("sweet place")
  158–159
team spirit 170–171
Thunderbird School of
  Management 20
tipping 157
titles 115–116, 121
toasting 127
todok (ethics)
  107–108
tomping ("dumping")
  207
tongchal yuk (keen
  insight) 63
tongchang hoe (alumni
  groups) 90
tongnip ("personal
  independence") 167
trust 135–136, 143,
  144–145
truth, situational
  83–84
  SEE ALSO *chongmal*

uimu (duty) 67–68
uiri (obligation) 67–68
uishin jonshin ("heart
  to heart") 88
Ulsan 15
undaeng i (rear end)
  207–208
unhye (benefits) 92
United Nations
United States 8, 13, 14,
  17, 36, 43, 44

"unrequited resent-
    ment" 23
vacation times 118
Veterans' Law
    171–172
violence 27–28, 58

Westernization 10, 37,
    59, 72
Whang, Dr. Il Chung
    147
"wide leg" 144
"winner takes all"
    attitude 151
wiom 146–147
women 41, 58, 110,

111, 120, 125,
136–137, 155, 201
and compliments 137
as managers 137
work ethic 26–27,
189
World War II 8, 29, 43
writing system 23–24,
39, 40

yangban 40, 208
yeon ("personal
    relations") 142–144
Yeongjong 15
yeui pomjol (etiquette)
66, 208

Yi dynasty, SEE Choson
    dynasty
Yi, Admiral Sun-Shin
    42
Yi, General Song-Gye
    40
Yoido 139–140
yojung (hostess house)
208
yonhoe (banquets) 208
yonjul ("connections")
72, 142–144
yuhaeng (fashion
    conscious) 209

zaibatsu 10, 12, 181

Published by Tuttle Publishing, an imprint
of Periplus Editions (HK) Ltd.

www.tuttlepublishing.com

ISBN 978-0-8048-4457-4

16 15 14
5 4 3 2 1   1401MP

Printed in Singapore

Distributors
North America, Latin America and Europe
Tuttle Publishing
364 Innovation Drive, North Clarendon,
VT 05759-9436 USA.
Tel: 1(802) 773-8930
Fax: 1(802) 773-6993
info@tuttlepublishing.com
www.tuttlepublishing.com

Japan
Tuttle Publishing
Yaekari Building, 3rd Floor, 5-4-12 Osaki,
Shinagawa-ku, Tokyo 141 0032
Tel: (81) 3 5437-0171
Fax: (81) 3 5437-0755
sales@tuttle.co.jp
www.tuttle.co.jp

Asia Pacific
Berkeley Books Pte. Ltd.
61 Tai Seng Avenue
#02-12, Singapore 534167
Tel: (65) 6280-1330
Fax: (65) 6280-6290
inquiries@periplus.com.sg
www.periplus.com

TUTTLE PUBLISHING® is a registered
trademark of Tuttle Publishing, a division
of Periplus Editions (HK) Ltd.

The Tuttle Story
"Books to Span the East and West"

Many people are surprised to learn
that the world's largest publisher
of books on Asia had its humble
beginnings in the tiny American
state of Vermont. The company's
founder, Charles Tuttle, belonged to
a New England family steeped in
publishing.

Immediately after WW II, Tuttle
served in Tokyo under General
Douglas MacArthur and was
tasked with reviving the Japanese
publishing industry. He later
founded the Charles E. Tuttle
Publishing Company, which thrives
today as one of the world's leading
independent publishers.

Though a westerner, Tuttle was
hugely instrumental in bringing a
knowledge of Japan and Asia to
a world hungry for information
about the East. By the time of his
death in 1993, Tuttle had published
over 6,000 books on Asian culture,
history and art—a legacy honored
by the Japanese emperor with the
"Order of the Sacred Treasure," the
highest tribute Japan can bestow
upon a non-Japanese.

With a backlist of 1,500 titles,
Tuttle Publishing is more active
today than at any time in its
past—inspired by Charles Tuttle's
core mission to publish fine books
to span the East and West and
provide a greater understanding
of each.